Unsubscribe From Anxiety

Opt out of the myth that worry is required
and take charge of your own life now

DAVID A. STONE

Unsubscribe From Anxiety

Opt out of the myth that worry is required
and take charge of your own life now

DAVID A. STONE

WINDWORD GROUP
PUBLISHING & MEDIA

The WindWord Group Publishing & Media
100 Bull Street, Suite 200
Savannah, GA 31401 USA
www.windwordgroup.com

Copyright © 2019 David A. Stone

All rights reserved.

No part of this book may be reproduced, scanned or distributed in printed or electronic form without permission.

ISBN-10: 1-947527-04-5
ISBN-13: 978-1-947527-04-1

Please contact the publisher regarding large-quantity book purchases, interviews or speaking requests.

Printed in the United States of America

To my readers
It's important to point out that there are many people who suffer debilitating anxiety as a result of very real mental illness. Nothing in this book is intended to suggest that fears, anxieties, or worries brought on by mental illness are self-created or simply habits of thinking. Nor am I suggesting that the methods described here are a substitute for professional medical care in those cases where it is required.

Warning!
Don't believe anything you read in this book. The techniques I share with you here have worked for me. Now I invite you to discover what is true and what works for you. Then, if it's true for you and works for you, I invite you to take these techniques, apply them in your life, share them, and work with them to make your life happier, less stressful, and more fulfilled.

Table of Contents

The Four Promises of This Book		1
It's Worth the Effort		11
Exercise 1 — Your Successes		*20*

Part 1 Why and How We Worry — 31

1	Understanding the Workings of Worry	32
2	You Were Trained to Worry	43
3	The Ups and Downs of Anxiety	52
4	The Structure of Worry	62
5	It's Just a Habit – and Habits can be Replaced	74
6	Bringing It On	84
7	You *Can* Stop Worrying	95

Part 2 Opting Out of Worry — 106

8	Taking 100 Percent Responsibility	107
	Exercise 2. Have To, Choose To	*118*
9	Raising Your Awareness	125
	Exercise 3. Can't or Won't	*138*
10	Taking Inventory	146
11	Letting Anxiety Go	159
12	What's the Worst That Could Happen?	170

Part 3	**Living a Worry-Free Life**	**179**
13	What Does Worry-Free Feel Like?	180
14	Worry-Free Habit #1: An Attitude of Gratitude	194
15	Worry-Free Habit #2: Replace It with Purpose	205
16	Worry-Free Habit #3: Instant Action	217
17	Ten New Mental Habits	230
18	What's Next?	244
Acknowledgments		253
About the Author		255

DAVID A. STONE

THE FOUR PROMISES OF THIS BOOK

I promise you four things from this book.

1. *I promise to show you that fear, anxiety, and worry are debilitating, yet highly removable, roadblocks that are preventing you from living your best life possible.*

It's been shown in study after study that anxiety and worry have significant ill effects on your body and your health. High blood pressure, increased heart rate, hyperventilation, weakness, fatigue, trouble concentrating, gastrointestinal problems, depression, muscle aches, and even loss of libido have all been linked to anxiety. Any of these conditions are not only painful, but also prevent you from living your life to the fullest. Want to go out and run in the yard with your kids? "Sorry, I'm feeling pretty low-energy today." Want to enjoy a date night at that new five-star restaurant? "Sorry, my stomach gets irritable and I have to be careful about what I eat." Want to curl up with that latest best-seller? "Sorry, I just can't seem to get my head to relax and enjoy a good book."

If fear is the number one thing that stops people from having the quality of life they dream of and deserve, what are your fears, your worries, and your anxieties preventing you from trying? From enjoying? From succeeding at? Do you really want to spend your life hiding behind the bushes, missing out on all the amazing opportunities and delights the world has to offer, simply because you're worried about . . .

Many people, as they approach the ends of their lives, have said that it's not the things they did that they regret. It's the things that they failed to try. Imagine your ninety-year-old self, having a conversation with today's self. What advice would that wise, elderly you provide? If you had a chance to leave worry and anxiety behind, would your ninety-year-old self advise you to go for it? Exactly!

2. *I promise to show you that anxiety and worry are simply mental and emotional choices that have become habits and that you are fully capable of replacing those habits with healthier, more constructive ones.*

Every single moment of every single day that we're alive and breathing, stuff is happening around us and to us. Some of that stuff is wonderful and fun and uplifting and delightful. Some of it is shitty.

For the most part, we have very little control over the things that happen to us and in the world around us. Bad weather is going to occasionally happen, regardless of how sunny our disposition might be. Some crackpot is going to shoot a gun, drive a car into a crowded sidewalk, or threaten to launch a missile, no matter what we might prefer. The economy is going to go up and then it's going to go down, without any respect for our retirement plans. We simply cannot control external events.

What we can control, however, is our response to and our thoughts regarding those events. When the Dow Jones or the NASDAQ drops five hundred points and the value of our mutual fund drops along with it, we have a choice: We can panic, worry that we'll be eating cat food in retirement, and lose even more sleep. Or we can remind ourselves that the economy goes up and down on a regular basis, reassure ourselves that our savings are being handled in the best possible way, and get on with enjoying our day. The choice is entirely up to us.

For our entire lives, though, the vast majority of the world around us has chosen the worry option. Observing how society typically reacts to bad news, we've been convinced and trained that there is something inherently correct in reacting anxiously, so we do it too. Choose this reaction often enough, over a long enough period of time, and it becomes a habit. Habits are behaviors that we've repeated so often and for so long that we no longer think about them. The behavior is automatic and even subconscious.

As we well know, not all habits are healthy and beneficial; entire industries and professions are built around helping people replace harmful habits with more beneficial ones. If you had the opportunity to give up a habit that made you ill, left you sleepless, and made it hard for you to concentrate, would you want to try? Exactly!

3. *I promise to show you how you can control your anxiety instead of it controlling you.*

Our brains are miraculous bits of biology: One hundred billion individual cells. One hundred trillion synapses, which are the minute gaps between the nerve cells. Impulses pass across these tiny gaps via neurotransmitters, allowing us to think thoughts, store memories, and figure stuff out.

We all think thousands of thoughts every day. None of the folks with fancy letters behind their names seem to agree on exactly how many; estimates range from twenty thousand to seventy thousand thoughts per day. Regardless, the scientists all agree that we think a lot. Among those tens of thousands of thoughts are some that can be categorized as worry, fear, anxiety, and self-doubt. For some people, the overwhelming majority of thoughts fall in those categories.

Sometimes it can feel as if you are absolutely consumed by anxiety and worry, especially when these frightening ideas become powerful enough to overwhelm other thoughts. It can feel as if they are an integral part of you, as if they actually *are* you. It can reach a stage where your worry affects every aspect of your life: You can't enjoy the activities you used to enjoy. You can't relax and unwind. It seems, sometimes, as if you can't even think rationally.

Your brain is the source of your thoughts and it's simply one of the many tools and resources you have at your disposal to make your way through life. Like your hands, your eyes, or your elbows, it's there to serve you. And just like your hands, eyes, and elbows, you're better off when you're in control of these valuable assets. Imagine if your eyes suddenly decided that they would choose what they wanted to look at and what they didn't. Life would be chaotic, and driving down the road would become much more dangerous.

When we allow our brains to be in charge of what we're thinking, life can be equally chaotic and out of control. You want to think relaxing thoughts, or your significant other wants to think romantic thoughts, but your brain has decided that you're going to worry about your finances. Again. Your kids want you to think about spending some play time with them, but your brain has decided that you should fret about what someone said on the neighborhood chat app.

Who's running the show here?!

If you found a way to be in control of your thoughts instead of them being in control of you, would you jump at it? Exactly!

4. I promise to give you proven, practical steps that will let you live the life you've always wanted to live.

As an anonymous, yet obviously wise person once observed, "Bad habits are like a comfortable bed, easy to get into, but hard to get out of." Because they require no effort on your part whatsoever, habits of thought can be even harder to get out of than behavioral ones. An old habit will only go away if we replace it with a new one. Once you've learned how to begin owning your thoughts instead of them owning you, you'll want to replace those old thought habits with new, healthy, strong and beneficial ones. Once those new, healthy habits of thought are in place, you'll wonder how you ever lived without them. Your life will truly transform before your eyes as challenges or events that once might have brought you to a standstill simply roll off your back. Some of the new habits that I'll be sharing with you will result in life changes that will feel almost miraculous. Things will begin to flow more smoothly for you. People you need to meet will mysteriously be brought into your life. Circumstances that are advantageous to you will crop up more often.

Sure, it might all seems a little woo-woo. But I'm here to report that it happens and it works. Don't ask me to explain how, I can't. Nor do I need to know. I don't know how magnets work, but that doesn't stop me from using one to stick my grocery list to the refrigerator. I don't know how gravity works, but I'm more than happy to let it hold my furniture down.

My point is, I'm coming to you from a place of personal experience. I used to lie awake at night, and now I sleep like a baby. I used to cringe whenever a bill showed up, and now I treat it like any other piece of useful, incoming information.

If you stumbled upon a method by which your life could be made easier, simpler, happier, and more joyous, would you want to try it, even if you couldn't explain how it worked? Exactly!

Here's a fifth, bonus promise: I promise that, if you follow these steps in a systematic way and commit yourself to replacing your old habits with the new ones I suggest, your worry and anxiety will diminish. They may not go completely away by the end of the process, but they absolutely will decrease and, eventually, perhaps sooner than you think possible, disappear altogether. Perhaps you even felt your first, small beginnings of transformation when you simply read the title of this book. Something deep inside you recognized that you *can* unsubscribe from anxiety. You *can* opt out of worry. The choice is absolutely yours.

If you'd like to be done with that nonstop, low-grade, chronic, "How-am-I-going-to-pay-the-cable-bill-this-month?", "Why-hasn't-my-friend-liked-my-Instagram-post-yet?", "I'm-sure-these-symptoms-mean-I-have-cancer!" kind of anxiety, this book has your answers. If you'd like to be done with that flavor of fear that comes late at night when you can't sleep and can't stop the tumbling cascade of imagined outcomes, you've opened the right book.

This book is going to show you how to stop worrying. It will show you how to untangle the net of fear and anxiety that keeps you from exploring and enjoying your limitless human potential and embracing the life you dream about.

In Part 1, we'll explore the ways in which the world conspires to keep us worrying and how we've fooled ourselves into believing that anxiety is normal. In Part 2, I'm going to show you that it's entirely within your power to turn your anxiety off and give you the techniques with which you can do this for yourself. Then, in Part 3, you'll learn the three keys to achieving your worry-free status plus a new set of mental habits that will help you maintain an anxiety-free life.

There are a number of exercises throughout this book, each designed to help you alter the way in which you see yourself and your worry habits. Several of the exercises include a form for your responses and you're welcome to use them. However, I highly recommend that you obtain a blank journal or notebook in which you can record your responses to the exercises as well as your evolving thoughts about your own anxieties. While it might be tempting to use a computer or tablet, I find that the slow, deliberate act of writing by hand rewards you with deeper contemplation and greater understanding of these concepts.

Think, for a moment, about how life would feel if you were absolutely free of worry and anxiety. What would you do if you weren't the least bit afraid to fail, succeed, change, be judged, look foolish, say 'no,' or try something completely different?

Let's find out.

IT'S WORTH THE EFFORT

Just like you, I was finally fed up with worrying. Worry is one of the most unpleasant emotions that you can experience as a human being, and I was experiencing it in glorious technicolor. I had the knots in my stomach, the aches in my head, and the lying awake at night, and I was tired of it all. But what bugged me the most was the sensation of what I call "looking down."

Mountain climbers and tightrope walkers are always instructed "not to look down." When you're clinging to the side of a cliff or balancing on a one-inch cable above Niagara Falls, a downward glance instantly and completely fills your mind with the horrific consequences of falling. Now, instead of envisioning your arms raised in victory at the summit, or the adulation of the media as you reach the far side, your only thoughts involve a hideous plunge to an even more hideous death. Now your every move is taken, not to achieve victory, but to avoid failure. In the world of competitive sports, you've shifted from playing to win to playing not to lose. And it never works.

Worry is like that. Instead of our minds focusing on joyous thoughts of career accomplishments, financial freedom, and loving relationships, we lie awake in the dark, roiling with the imagined ignominy of joblessness, bankruptcy, and abandonment. Try as we might, we can't shake those ominous thoughts about the failure, loss, and catastrophe that appear to be looming over our heads, about to crush us at any moment.

Yeah, I was fed up with worrying. So I decided to quit.

I know that you, also, want to surrender your membership in the Worry-of-the-Day Club, unsubscribe from anxiety, and opt out of the myth that worry has to be a fact of life. And you can. It is well within your ability, without the use of medication or expensive therapy. Because the truth is that fear, worry, and anxiety do *not* need to be a part of your life. You *can* live a life that is driven by your dreams. You *can* wake up every morning, excited with the promise of the new day. You *can* leave worry behind and still deal with all the challenges that life loves to throw at you. All this is entirely in your hands and within your power. All it takes is a choice. Your choice.

What are my credentials for being able to show you how to abandon anxiety? I'm a world-class expert in both worrying and leaving it behind.

My worry training began early in life, many decades before social media even existed. The household in which I grew up wasn't technically poor, but the ratio of money to kids was certainly at the low end of the scale. Once a month, I watched my parents sit at the kitchen table with the bills spread out in front of them as they performed the monthly juggling act between a lean bank account and a fat pile of bills. They were raised during the Depression and had favorite phrases such as "robbing Peter to pay Paul," and "trying to make a silk purse out of a sow's ear." The very words spoken at the table during those sessions spoke of scarcity, impending disaster, and looming calamity.

I learned early to believe that money is hard to come by and that being rich was reserved for the lucky or the crooked. I carried that erroneous belief into adulthood and lay awake way too many nights worrying about whether or not I'd be able to meet next month's car payment, cable bill, and mortgage installment.

The interesting thing was, there was always enough money and I've never actually missed a mortgage payment. While my anxiety had nothing to do with objective reality, that fact didn't make it go away. "Sure, I'm good for this month. But what about *next* month!?"

Of course money, or rather the lack of it, is just one of the more popular worry topics. There are plenty of others. Writing in Psychology Today, Graham C.L. Davey Ph.D. claims that worries fall into a number of different domains, including relationships, work, finances, future direction, and lack of confidence. Others chunk it down into four major categories—money and the future, job security, relationships, and health. When the British publication *indy100* asked two thousand people what they worried about most, they came up with the following list.

20. The area I live in/crime levels
19. Pet's health
18. If my dress sense is good
17. Meeting work targets or goals
16. Whether I'm a good parent/raising kids right
15. A friend or family member I've fallen out with
14. Whether I'll find the right partner/whether my current partner is right
13. Whether my partner still loves me
12. Whether or not I am attractive
11. I need to find a new job
10. I seem to be generally unhappy

9. Paying rent/mortgage
8. Worried about my physique
7. Wrinkles or ageing appearance
6. Job security
5. Financial/credit card debts
4. My diet
3. Low energy levels
2. Worried about my savings/financial future
1. Getting old in general

Of course this is hardly a scientific study and please don't start worrying if your particular worries aren't on the list or your top five are different. How ironic is it that we are capable of worrying that we're worrying too much!

Regardless of what we find ourselves anxious about, sooner or later we decide that it's too much.

In August of 2009 I was 55 years old, an internationally known marketing consultant making a healthy six-figure income and living in my car. Not the 'living in my car' as in the road warrior who keeps Hertz in business, but literally, every night pulling into the same highway rest stop, grabbing the pillow out of the back seat, and spending the night with my leg wrapped over the gearshift.

How did I get there? I'd spent the previous 30 years worrying and fretting about everything. On the outside I appeared like a successful, easy-going businessman. But inside, regardless of how well I was doing, it was never enough. From that early training around the kitchen table I learned and firmly believed that it would eventually run out. And so it did.

As life goes on, the Universe tends to nudge us with hints and suggestions towards success. It wants desperately to hand us those life hacks that result in the shortcuts to success and happiness. I'd clearly been ignoring the nudges and had found neither. When the Universe finally decides that we've ignored its subtle hints long enough, it eventually smacks us upside the head with a 2x4. Sometimes it's a heart attack. Sometimes it's a divorce. Sometimes it's bankruptcy. There's no end to the disasters that can be cleverly used to get your attention.

For me, it was homelessness. For the first time in my life I was backed into a corner with no choice but to admit that doing things 'my way' was not producing the results that I wanted. I clearly recall sitting in the car very early one morning. The sun was just coming up through the pine trees and the big rigs that had also spent the night at the truck stop were firing up their diesels. I looked around, assessed my situation, and said, out loud, to whoever might be listening, *"I give up! My way is clearly not working and I'm wide open to hearing about and trying some better ideas!"*

I spent the next five years learning everything I could about how our minds and our thoughts work, how they affect our lives, and how we can learn to control them instead of them controlling us. I studied and practiced how to choose my thoughts, how to observe them in a detached, objective way, how to shut them off when I wished and, significantly, how to recognize when my thoughts were not serving my better interests.

I deconstructed fear into its many component parts, some of which prove to be quite useful, others downright limiting and debilitating. I learned that worry and anxiety were among the latter and that they were not the least bit useful in living a full, joyous, and purposeful life. So I learned to set them aside and leave them behind. I can now honestly say, to both you and to myself in the mirror, that I live a worry-free life. And it feels so freaking good that I simply have to share the "how" of it all with you.

Now, technically, that previous bit about "I've-never-actually-missed-a-mortgage-payment" isn't true. In 2006 I got caught in the earliest stages of the Great Recession with a house in Chicago that I couldn't give away, let alone sell at a price that would allow me to pay off the bank. Because I'd already moved and bought another house, I defaulted on that mortgage and the bank foreclosed. In other words, my worst possible fears, that I'd been harboring since childhood, actually came true. (We'll talk more about that dynamic later.)

It turned out, though, that those worst possible outcomes weren't that horrible after all. Yes, it was inconvenient. Yes, it was embarrassing. But I lived to tell about it and I didn't end up dead or in some hellhole prison with rats and a once-a-day bowl of gruel.

The point is, our worst suffering lies in the worry and anxiety itself. The outcomes we dread almost never turn out to be the hideous nightmares we imagine. There is an old saying, attributed, among others, to Thomas Jefferson; "My life has been full of terrible misfortunes most of which never happened." Or, as Franklin D. Roosevelt famously said at the height of the Great Depression, "The only thing we have to fear is fear itself—nameless, unreasoning, unjustified terror which paralyzes needed efforts to convert retreat into advance."

There are so many good reasons to leave worry and anxiety behind: restlessness, increased blood pressure, trouble concentrating, and irritability to name just a few. But in my opinion, there are two enormous, overwhelming reasons to choose to unsubscribe from anxiety. The first is that it never, ever helps the situation. You can stay up all night for a week worrying yourself sick, and the situation about which you're anxious won't change one whit. It simply doesn't help. For all the mental and emotional energy you're investing, you'd think that something positive would come out. But it never does. Problem solving is a good thing. Worry is not.

The second—and, in my opinion, the most significant—reason to opt out of worry is that anxiety prevents you from rising to your highest potential. When you spend your life looking down, you're never able to look up, see, and then reach for the glorious things that you and your life can become. When fear, anxiety, and self-doubt are in control, it's impossible for you to become your highest, most wondrous self.

We've snagged ourselves in a net of fretfulness. We've hijacked our own imaginations, psyches, and inner monologues and turned them against ourselves. We have immobilized ourselves through an addiction to twenty-four-hour news, social media, and the opinions of others. We live in fear, yet we can't seem to look away and release ourselves from the addiction to an endless barrage of negativity couched in ever-rising hyperbole.

And while our imaginations, our psyches, and

our inner monologues have been hijacked, so too has our precious supply of human energy and potential. As author and motivational speaker Tony Robbins has said, "The number one thing that stops people from having the quality of life they want and deserve is fear."

It is entirely possible to eradicate anxiety and worry from your life. You won't do it in a day, and it will require some concentrated effort on your part. But I promise you that your results, your quality of life, your daily experience of joy and contentment will be absolutely worth the effort.

Exercise #1
Your Successes

Whenever you head out on a journey it's smart to take along a few supplies. Whether it's some water on an afternoon hike or a map and some snacks on a road trip, a few basic provisions are indispensable along the way.

As we go through this book together, we'll be heading down a road that will lead us to being less fearful, less anxious, less worried, and less self-doubting. But let's face it, we're not there yet. We'll have to take a journey to get from our current place of anxiety to that land of fearlessness. What are the supplies we'll need to get us all the way there?

Fearlessness is built on confidence, which is built on self-esteem. And self-esteem is built when one small accomplishment is stacked on another and then another. Every time we achieve a goal, win a victory, or pull off an achievement, our self-esteem grows. We feel better about ourselves and we're more willing to take on the next challenge.

Things get sticky, though, when obstacles come along and our anxieties and self-doubts fill the windshield again. When that happens, the self-esteem disappears and it seems like we're back to square one. That's why it's important to bring a knapsack full of victories, accomplishments, and achievements along for this journey. That's why it's vital to head out onto this road with our heads filled with the successes and victories that you've already achieved.

When we're anxious, our thoughts on those worry topics crowd out every other thought we might want to have. Have you ever noticed, when you're in a bad mood, and someone attempts to cheer you up, it often simply annoys you more? "Don't bother me with your stupid platitudes about 'This too shall pass,' or 'Look on the bright side!' Can't you see that I'm busy being miserable?!" When we're worried, our minds are so wrapped up with the impending doom that there is simply no room for anything else.

Fortunately, this strategy works in the other direction too. When our minds are so filled with self-esteem and pride in our accomplishments, there is no room for anxiety. So we're going to begin this process by recalling and documenting the amazing achievements of your life so far. The fact that you are here today, alive and breathing, is proof that you have overcome every single challenge that life has thrown at you so far. If you hadn't, you'd be dead. (Of course, on the bright side, if you were dead, you wouldn't be worried. But since we'd rather be both alive and unworried, let's carry on.)

It's far too easy, in the face of anxiety, to forget

that you've had countless successes in your life so far. From the youngest age when you first learned to walk, talk, and dispense with the need for diapers, you've been scoring win after win. We tend not to think of our accomplishments as victories, but each achievement is a mark in your 'W' column and it's extremely helpful to regularly review your performance.

Start by making a list—it *must* be written—of five things you did before you were eighteen that you were really proud of. It doesn't matter how big or small they seem now; they were big to you at the time. Perhaps you caught a fly ball in Little League. Or maybe you stood up in front of your sixth-grade class and read a poem you'd written. I remember, at about age twelve or thirteen, building a go-cart from bits and pieces of scrap metal and an old lawnmower motor that my dad had in the garage. My today-self can see it as a rusty pile of junk, held together by bits of wire, but I'll never forget the incredible feeling when it actually ran and I was bumping noisily around the front yard.

What about you? What were some of your earliest accomplishments? Review the various categories, including sports, academics, your social life, skills you acquired, and challenges you overcame. One woman won her regional swimming meet as a teenager. Did you earn a merit badge in your Scout troop? Make the honor roll? Jump off the high board at the local pool?

As you add each success to the list, close your eyes and remember how you felt at the time of that victory. Put yourself back into that feeling place for a few moments and let yourself glow with pride all over again.

It's remarkable how, when we're so wrapped up in worry, it becomes difficult, if not impossible, to recall anything you've done that's worthy of pride. We have to train ourselves to focus on those victories and achievements, to bring them easily to mind and to experience, again, the wonderful feelings of pride, of accomplishment, and of worthiness that accompany them. This exercise begins to stretch and strengthen our anti-anxiety muscles and builds a more balanced mental and emotional outlook.

I'm proud of these five successes that I achieved before I turned eighteen:

1. _____
   _____

I recall feeling:
_____
_____

2. _____
_____

I recall feeling:

_____
_____

3. _____
_____

I recall feeling:

_____
_____

4. _____
_____

I recall feeling:

_____
_____

5. _____
_____

I recall feeling:

_____
_____

Next, make a list of five things you accomplished in college or at your very first job. Again, they don't have to be huge in your eyes today. What matters is that they were victories to you at the time. Perhaps it was getting accepted at a tough-to-get-into school. Maybe it was being elected to a student body or scoring a high mark on an exam or term paper.

If you're thinking about your first job, recall the feeling you had when you first found out that you'd been hired. Or the thrill of successfully completing an assignment that was a challenge to you. Perhaps it was the feeling you had in a performance review meeting that ended with you receiving a raise.

Whether it was school or work, the challenges you overcame in those moments seemed daunting, even overwhelming in their time, but somehow you found the courage and the determination to do it anyway.

Take a moment to pat yourself on the back again today for that wins you scored back then. And, as an important part of this exercise, put yourself back into the elated, triumphant, and self-satisfied feelings that you experienced in the moments and days following your achievements.

I'm proud of these five successes that I achieved in college or at my first job:

1. _____
   _____

I recall feeling:

_____
_____

2. _____
   _____

I recall feeling:

_____
_____

3. _____
   _____

I recall feeling:

_____
_____

4. _____
   _____

I recall feeling:

_____

_____

5. _____

_____

I recall feeling:

_____

_____

You can repeat this exercise for as many time periods in your life as you'd like, and I highly recommend it. Perhaps move through your life in five- or ten-year increments, making lists of the victories, achievements, and high points that you've accomplished along the way. In each instance, put yourself back into the emotional place that felt so good, so empowering, so worthy following that win. This helps you establish new emotional habits and get used, once again, to the feeling that you have when things are going right and the future holds nothing but the promise of more.

Regardless of how many life segments you review, make sure you create a list of five successes you had last week. It might take some thinking because we've gotten into the habit of focusing on the things that haven't or might not work out. But they're there. In a recent workshop, one woman was completely unable to recall anything in the past week that she could categorize as a shining moment. With a little coaching, however, she began to recognize the highlights of her days when she shared lunch with a friend, enjoyed a conversation with her daughter, and stumbled upon a bargain while shopping. When our minds are preoccupied with worry, it takes a little practice to see the shiny bits.

For you, it might be a great meal that you cooked, a really insightful report you wrote, or the way you brought a smile to someone else. Each one is a victory, an accomplishment, a win. And each time we bring these wins back into our minds, our self-esteem grows. The more our self-esteem grows, the more confident we become, the more willing we are to try something new and different and challenging. And every time we try and succeed at something that's new and challenging, the closer we get to fearlessness.

I really enjoyed these five bright spots in just the past week:

1. _____
   _____

I recall feeling:
_____
_____

2. _____
_____

I recall feeling:
_____
_____

3. _____
_____

I recall feeling:
_____
_____

4. _____
_____

I recall feeling:
_____
_____

5. _____
_____

I recall feeling:

_____

_____

Healthy confidence and self-esteem are built on the successes and accomplishments that we've achieved. In order to build self-esteem, we need to regularly remind ourselves of our successes and remember that, more often than not, we triumph over the challenges that life puts in front of us.

When you're facing a challenge that seems daunting, it's too easy to forget the things you've already accomplished, the challenges you've already overcome, and the bad-ass warrior that you actually are. So when you head out on the road towards fearlessness, be sure to bring along a big supply of previous victories.

Part 1 — Why and How We Worry

In this part you're going to get in behind the curtain of anxiety and worry.

This is important because, before you can achieve mastery over it and leave it behind, it's necessary to fully understand why and how you started to be anxious in the first place, the benefits (yes, there are a couple) and drawbacks of worry, and how anxiety and self-doubt work in your mind.

This process of studying, in a detached, objective way, allows you to see that your worry isn't, in fact, an integral part of who you are. It's simply a habit of thinking that you've acquired over the years. Like any habit, once you've decided that you'd be better off without it, you can set about replacing it with better, healthier, and more constructive habits.

1

UNDERSTANDING THE WORKINGS OF WORRY

If you know the enemy and know yourself, you need not fear the result of a hundred battles. If you know yourself but not the enemy, for every victory gained you will also suffer a defeat. If you know neither the enemy nor yourself, you will succumb in every battle.

—Sun Tzu, *The Art of War*

The *Art of War* was written more than 2,500 years ago by a Chinese general named Sun Tzu. While it has long been studied and lauded for its advice on success on the military battlefield, it has more recently been seized on by countless entrepreneurs and businesspeople looking for an edge in the corporate world.

His advice to know the enemy is enormously valuable to us as we begin the process of overcoming anxiety and leaving worry behind. If we don't understand how worry works or the structure of anxiety, how can we ever possibly hope to achieve victory over them?

In this section you're going to become a worry expert.

I can hear you now: "I'm already a worry expert! I'm so good at it that I could win a world champion worry contest! I want to *stop* worrying, not get to know it even more intimately!"

While it likely feels as if you've been up close and personal with worry for far too long already, we're talking about a different kind of expertise. Instead of being an expert in how to worry, I want you to master the intricacies of how worry and anxiety actually work in your brain, what brings them on, what they're actually made of, and what makes them tick.

I want you to think of yourself as a scientist in a laboratory. You're wearing a white lab coat and you're about to conduct an academic study of this new subject of yours called 'Anxiety.' There's a big blob of it sitting on your laboratory bench and you're going to measure it, probe it, take its temperature, weigh it, and learn everything there is to know about this mysterious creature.

Like any good scientist, you're going to bring a very detached, objective approach to this study.

You'll experience neither attachment to nor revulsion from your subject. You're going to be a neutral, third-party observer viewing it at a distance, examining it, analyzing it, dissecting, and understanding it in an impersonal, clinical way. Only then will you be able to decide what you want to do with it.

The first thing we're going to learn is that we live in a world that seems designed to make us anxious. We are completely surrounded and constantly inundated by events, circumstances, media, and people who seem hell-bent on having us worry.

There have always been conditions that conspired to make humans anxious and afraid. From the saber-toothed tiger lurking outside the cave, to the Black Plague, to being drafted and shipped off to the jungles of Vietnam, there's never a shortage of things to keep us awake at night. But during the last couple of decades we seem to have brought anxiety to a high rolling boil and perfected the art of allowing perceived, yet intangible, threats to immobilize us.

Let's begin at the level of the solar system—yes, there is even bad news to worry about there!

As I write, CNN is reporting that an Israeli spacecraft, intended for a soft lunar landing, didn't land so softly. In fact it crashed on the moon. While that's bad news for the project's backers, we're told that its payload included thousands of tiny, millimeter-long bugs that were chosen specifically because of their ability to survive. Among the most resilient forms of life known, they can survive radiation, the vacuum of space, and even, to quote one of the mission's co-founders, "practically any planetary cataclysm." And now they're splashed across the surface of the moon.

While we're still up there in orbit, let's tune in to The Weather Channel's regular program *Deadliest Space Weather*, which is sure to calm you into a relaxed, meditative state.

Back here on earth, I was walking through an airport recently while being bombarded by TV monitors blaring CNN and Fox News's versions of our daily Armageddon. Climate change, the most recent mass shooting, fires in California, earthquakes in Central America, raging partisanship in Washington and London, and another crackpot dictator threatening to rain missiles down on his target-de-jour.

Just for fun, let's throw in terrorism, the price of real estate, and the various whack-jobs who've been elected or have appointed themselves to run the place. All of this hosted by news anchors who are paid to increase our sense of urgency with intro lines such as, "Here's what you need to know—*RIGHT NOW.*"

The truth is, you don't need to know most of the content of the news. And you certainly don't need to know it *RIGHT NOW*. While it's one thing to remain an informed citizen, it's another to invite constant exposure to news content that will have zero direct impact on you. With the important exception, of course, of raising your anxiety levels and blood pressure.

Would you like to simply check on tomorrow's weather to see if the family reunion should be indoors or out? Not quite so simple or worry-free as it ought to be. The Weather Channel has mastered the questionable art of writing terror-inducing headlines:

"Incoming Threat: Strong to Severe Storms"
"'Ring of Fire' Weather Pattern Brings Heat Wave, Thunderstorms"
"Entire Busy Intersection Suddenly Ignites" (complete with video)
"Hurricane Central: El Niño Has Ended and That Could Have a Huge Impact"
"More Than a Dozen Dead as Typhoon Strikes"
"34 People Killed in Landslide"

And the sensationalism isn't just restricted to the current weather. When it's not reporting today's thunderstorm in Topeka, The Weather Channel has to fill twenty-four hours with eyeball-grabbing programs. What better way to grab lots of attention and lots of advertising revenue that to have regular programming with titles like *Why Planes Crash, So You Think You'd Survive?, Strangest Weather on Earth, It Could Happen Tomorrow,* and *Forecasting the End,* just to name a few current and previous shows.

And, why have us cringe in fear from just one tornado show, when we can have three! *Tornado 360, Tornado Alley,* and *Tornado Road.*

Most of our worries and anxieties, however, are much closer to home. We worry about paying the cable bill next month, whether that mole on your arm is getting any bigger, why my friend hasn't liked my Instagram post, what your mother will say if you go to Vegas with that guy for the weekend, and whether or not you can win that rare spot in the best pre-K so your three-year-old will get into Yale. All these contribute to that special flavor of fear that comes late at night when you can't sleep and can't stop the tumbling cascade of imagined outcomes about to befall you.

Here's how worry unfolds, with the enthusiastic assistance of the world around us:

It's an absolutely perfect day. My wife and I are on board the **Queen Mary 2***, sailing from Hamburg,*

Germany to New York, having just enjoyed a six-week sabbatical in Europe while she works on her writing and I collect my thoughts as I get ready to write this book. We're in the ship's library—a beautiful, quiet place with burled walnut paneling, stacks and stacks of delicious books, and a calming view of the ocean. We've just had a delightful breakfast, I'm in the zone, and the ideas are flowing.

Then, from behind me, someone coughs. Not a long, hacking kind of cough, just one of those polite little, clear-your-throat things that we all do occasionally. But instantly, my mind pictures the many posters around the ship reminding us all to wash our hands regularly to avoid norovirus.

Norovirus is a highly contagious, rather unpleasant illness of the stomach or intestines causing vomiting and diarrhea. Anyone can catch it from direct contact with an infected person, consuming contaminated food or water, or touching a contaminated surface then putting your unwashed hands in your mouth. Symptoms usually develop within twelve to forty-eight hours after exposure, and most people get better within one to three days. According to the Centers for Disease Control, there are 685 million cases reported globally each year, resulting in 200,000 deaths—less than three one-hundredths of one percent of the total number of people who fall ill. In other words, your likely worst outcome is a couple of days spent close to a bathroom.

As much as you don't want to get norovirus, cruise ship companies don't want you to get it even more. It's bad for business. Remember that awful Samuel L. Jackson movie *Snakes on a Plane*? It took advantage of some of our worst fears—deadly reptile, enclosed space, nowhere to run . . . It's the stuff nightmares are made of, and it's designed to sell theater tickets. A cruise ship company, on the other hand, wants you to enthusiastically get on board. And the last thing they want is for you to imagine some hideous deadly virus in their floating enclosed space, with nowhere for you to run. So they go out of their way to reassure you of their cleanliness procedures, their safety records, and your need to wash your hands.

In 2018, 27.2 million people took cruises. Of the roughly three hundred cruise ships operating around the world, exactly five reported norovirus outbreaks in 2018. While the few outbreaks that do occur aboard cruise ships always make the headlines and make it seem like they're on the rise, they're no more prevalent today than they were in the 1990s and 2000s. There's just a higher awareness because the media can't resist a great terror-inducing story about a large number of people in a confined space with an infection that spreads so easily.

When it comes to a showdown between the media and the cruise line's reassurance though, all their precautions can't stop my fertile mind. The worry seed has been planted:

What if the cougher is sick? What if the air in this library isn't fresh enough? It's awfully stuffy in here! I didn't get the vaccination! I bet this slight tickle in my own throat is the beginnings of it. What are the symptoms of norovirus? How many people get it every year? Aren't ships and confined spaces where it's known to spread like wildfire?! Why did they let that guy on the ship at all? I bet I've got it now. How long do I have to live? Will my final weeks be spent in hideous suffering? Why haven't they found a cure for this already?! What's wrong with those medical people anyway, don't they see what an epidemic this is!?

The media and our vivid imaginations both love the drama.

Hans Rosling was a Swedish physician, academic, and statistician who died in 2017. His posthumously published book *Factfulness: Ten Reasons We're Wrong about the World—and Why Things Are*

Better Than You Think, written with Ola Rosling and Anna Rosling Rönnlund, talks about what he calls the "overdramatic worldview." While it's easy to blame the media for over-dramatization, Rosling's research led him to conclude that it comes from the very way our brains work. The brain is a product of millions of years of evolution, and we are hardwired with instincts that seek out drama, which helped our ancestors to survive. He advises that now, in our twenty-first-century world, we need to learn to control our drama intake.

The media and activists rely on drama to grab your attention. Negative stories are more dramatic than positive ones, and it's far simpler and more headline-grabbing to report a story about crisis that is, in fact, an anomaly in the context of a long-term improvement. Take a look at these headlines from the first half of 2019, for example:

- Population Doubles For One of New Zealand's Rarest Birds, As 150 Chicks Hatch This Season
- Scientists Are 'Thrilled' to Report That Hawaiian Coral Reefs Are Finally Stabilizing After Mass Bleaching
- Global Suicide Rate Has Declined By 29 percent, With Millions of Tragedies Avoided Since 2000
- US Cancer Death Rate Has Fallen by 27 percent in 25 Years — Study

- Suicide Rate Among UK Men at Lowest in 30 Years
- No Rise in Autism in Past Three Years, Says Large U.S. Study
- India Has Saved Thousands of Lives by Increasing Sanitation Coverage from 40 percent to 90 percent in Just Four Years

There is no doubt that there are nasty things going on in the world. Only a fool with their head in the sand would deny it. But if you only paid attention to the 24/7 news outlets, you'd be led to believe that nothing but bad things are going on. It is not your imagination—the media outlets are purposely working to raise the drama quotient and own your eyeballs for even more hours every day. Why? So they can sell more ads to the pharmaceutical companies who want you to ask your doctor if DramApocalypse is right for you.

As we get to "know the enemy" and their plans to occupy our unconscious minds, let's impose some filters on what we pay attention to and begin to recognize what's being done to us.

2

YOU WERE TRAINED TO WORRY

Let's stay in the laboratory and go even deeper with our objective, scientific inquiry into the nature and origins of our worries and self-doubts. You may be surprised to find that many of them weren't even your idea in the first place.

At a recent workshop, one woman talked about how her mother is a worrier, her sister is a worrier and, in fact, everyone around her is a worrier. Many, if not most of us, grew up around at least someone who was a worrier, and it couldn't help but rub off. One person I know can't go on a road trip without fretting about the route they'll take, if they're driving too fast, what the distance to the next gas station might be, and whether or not the car will break down.

For way too many people, worry and anxiety are the normal, default conditions. The phone rings and you assume it's someone calling with bad news. There's a knock at the door and your first thought is that it's the police, coming to inform you that your son has been in an accident. The school sends a note home with your child and, before you've even opened it, you're convinced it has to do with a behavior problem.

Why do our minds always and immediately go to the worst possible negative outcome? Why doesn't my mind, instead, respond, "I bet it's Publishers Clearing House with my million-dollar check!" Or, "They probably want him to represent the school at the United Nations!" Why do we imagine all the things that could go wrong but never give equal time to consider, list, and weigh everything that could go right? Why is our default position always to instantly imagine all the horrible outcomes that are likely to befall us?

Turns out that there are two reasons for this.

The first is that our brains are naturally wired with something called a 'negativity bias.' This means that, through millions of years of evolution, our brains have grown to be more sensitive to bad news than good. In studies conducted at Ohio State University, neuroscientist John Cacioppo showed that our brains react more strongly to negative stimuli than to positive ones. Our attitudes are more influenced by bad news than by good.

It makes sense too. When we were wandering around in the same neighborhood as hungry saber-toothed tigers, we were well served by a brain with systems that made us notice, and respond, to danger. Today, the tigers are long gone but that biology is still with us. Now, instead of noticing a charging mastodon, our negativity bias is alerting us to the insulting Facebook post or the (extremely remote) possibility of a bad medical diagnosis. As Hara Estroff Marano wrote in *Psychology Today*, "Nastiness just makes a bigger impact on our brains."

The second reason is that, from our earliest years, we've been trained and conditioned to worry.

And I do mean earliest! Numerous scientific studies indicate that anxiety in the mother during pregnancy can have significant mental and behavioral effects on the child as it grows up. The results of one study showed that high levels of maternal anxiety have a "significant relation with mental disorders, emotional problems, lack of concentration and hyperactivity and impaired cognitive development of children." The same study also concluded that anxiety during pregnancy can lead to "irritability and restlessness, individual differences in reaction to stressful life events and more fear in dealing with life events." Another study concluded that both physiological and emotional/mental effects of prenatal anxiety continue into infancy and childhood. On the mental/emotional side, effects can include "greater negative emotionality and in infants, lower mental development scores and internalizing problems. Anxiety disorders occur during childhood and elevated cortisol and internalizing behaviors occur during adolescence."

None of this means, however, that you can't lessen your own anxiety levels. In fact, simply knowing the origins of your own unease begins to make it far easier to walk away from it.

Perhaps your mother was completely Zen-like during her pregnancy, and you emerged as balanced and unblemished as can be. Immediately, and rightly, your parents began to look after and protect you.

Think about the advice that all caring parents give to their children: "Don't talk to strangers!" "Don't forget to wash your hands—you don't want to get sick." "Be careful on the way home from school." "Your hand will turn green and fall off if you keep doing that!"

To be sure, the advice about not talking to strangers is excellent—when you're eight years old and walking home from school alone. But when you're twenty-six or fifty-six and still cringing when someone you don't know walks up and rings your doorbell, things are out of control. While it's good that our parents taught us to be cautious, they should also have taught us when it's okay to back off on the yellow alerts. All the admonitions taught us to be basically untrusting and wary of the world around us.

It's also a very good idea to wash your hands regularly. But when you carry a bottle of hand sanitizer everywhere you go, wiping down every surface you plan to touch, it's reached a level of anxiety that borders on paranoia. Our biology provides us with an immune system that's designed to filter out the germs without any help from Purell. In fact, your immune system needs to encounter and learn about new bacteria all the time if it's to remain robust and effective. If we're constantly killing off all the germs on the shopping cart handle before our bodies have a chance to learn how to deal with them, we weaken our immune systems' ability to ward off disease. Then, like the Mayans, Incas, and Aztecs when they encountered the first Europeans, our bodies won't stand a chance to fend for themselves when some new virus sneaks past the sanitizer.

We also like to pass along our personal paranoias. Among the most common phobias are fears of spiders, snakes, flying, dogs, needles, germs, and heights. A parent who has their own particular fear of dogs, for example, is very likely to insist that his or her children should stay away from them and fill their young minds with all the terrible things that are likely to happen should they encounter a dog. As a result, the otherwise normally balanced child grows up believing that dogs (or airplanes or doctor's needles or tall buildings) are to be avoided at all costs. The fears are irrational, but the training is effective nonetheless.

In addition to instilling fears and phobias, our early training by parents, teachers, coaches, and others in authority established a limiting set of beliefs and self-doubts that continue to hinder our growth well into, or even throughout, our adult lives. We have been buried under an avalanche of "sensibles," "shoulds," "ought tos," and "you'd betters" that told us, repeatedly, that our deepest and most precious desires were somehow wrong, misguided, or stupid.

Every infant knows exactly what it wants and doesn't hesitate to ask for it. You knew the foods you liked and spit out the ones you didn't. You knew when you wanted to sleep and when you wanted to be held. When you become mobile, you saw what you wanted and headed straight for it. And that's when the admonitions began:

Don't touch that!

Keep your hands to yourself.

Eat everything on your plate.

You don't really feel that way.
You don't really want that.
You should be ashamed of yourself!
Stop crying. Don't be such a baby.

As you got older it morphed into . . .
You can't have everything you want simply because you want it.
Money doesn't grow on trees.
Stop being so selfish!
Stop doing what you are doing and come do what I want you to do!

It doesn't take too much of this before you throw up your hands and conclude that your desires, your wishes, your preferences don't matter. Why bother with them at all? It's a waste of time and emotional energy to have dreams of your own. The secret, it turned out, was to figure out what everybody else wanted you to do. To learn to please others and find ways to get their approval, whether it made you feel good or not.
You became an engineer because that's what Dad wanted you to do.
You married that guy because everybody else was getting married.
You became a lawyer because everyone said that you'd never make a living as an artist.

You became so sensible that you completely lost touch with who you really are and what you really want. And in the process, you took on one of the biggest and most common worries of all: What do other people think of me?

From the point of your conception to this very moment, the world around you has been teaching you to worry and doubt yourself. Everybody else worries, so it only makes sense that you should too. There's even a so-called joke that goes something like, "If you're not worried, it's because you haven't realized how bad things are." Or, as Joseph Heller wrote in *Catch-22*, "Just because you're paranoid doesn't mean they aren't after you."

We see worry all around us every day. Our common language encourages us to worry with phrases such as, "Oh, that's worrisome!" "Mom is worried about you." "I'd be worried if I were you." We read about worry and are told that we ought to worry about (insert the concern-du-jour here). It's assumed that we're supposed to worry, and we don't ever question the wisdom of worrying. After all, it's a time-honored practice.

Take a few minutes and think back to your childhood, your youth, and your adulthood. You might find it useful to journal a few of your thoughts about the origins of your own worry habits.

How were you taught to worry?
What were you told?
What did you observe?
How did some of your childhood, teenage, and young adult experiences launch or reinforce any worry habits?
How did any of those experiences initiate any self-doubts you might have?

Yes, we've been attending worry lessons our entire lives. But in all that time, no one has ever pointed out the simple truth that worry doesn't help anything. Nothing has ever changed as a result of worrying about it. We worry because we have been conditioned to do so. A newborn has an instinctive fear of falling and of loud noises. Everything else is learned and conditioned.

You learned how to worry. Now it's time to unlearn it.

3

THE UPS AND DOWNS OF ANXIETY

If a problem is fixable, if a situation is such that you can do something about it, then there is no need to worry. If it's not fixable, then there is no help in worrying. There is no benefit in worrying whatsoever.

—Dalai Lama

As we continue our objective study of worry and anxiety, it makes sense that we examine the advantages and disadvantages that it offers. As with any habit, even the damaging ones, a reasonable person will only continue in that habit if there is a payoff of some sort.

The smoker might believe it makes them appear cool or rebellious. They might also decide that the joy of the nicotine hit outweighs the effort of withdrawal. The heavy drinker might find it easier to socialize when under the influence or decide that the ability to temporarily escape from life's challenges makes the health risks seem worthwhile.

What, if any, might be the payoffs for continuing to worry? Turns out that there are a few, some of which might be seen as genuine benefits. The majority, though, start to seem a bit of a stretch when viewed in the cold light of the laboratory. But we need to know everything we can about this thing that so incessantly occupies our minds.

The fact that I worry shows others that I care about them.
Some people enjoy the role of "Official Worrier." Whether it's in a family, a group of friends, or a business, the designated worrier often relishes their role of watching out for trouble.

Worrying is my way of solving problems.
People who enjoy worrying often believe that, if something is wrong, it will require a great deal of thought if it's to be fixed. Worrying about a problem makes them believe it's more likely to be solved.

Worrying keeps me motivated.
Of course, there are other, perhaps better, ways to stay motivated, but the habitual worrier might believe that worrying about money motivates them

to become more financially informed or that worrying about their health motivates them to maintain a healthy lifestyle.

When I worry ahead of time, I keep bad things from happening.
This belief might lead you to think that worrying will help you stave off otherwise inevitable maladies or disasters. "Everything is going well for us financially because I constantly worry about going broke. If I didn't worry at it, we'd be making bad money decisions."

When I worry, I'm much more likely to take action.
This is actually one of the few potentially real benefits of anxiety. If a problem is serious enough, and if the worrier hasn't become trapped and paralyzed by worry, an action orientation provides real problem-solving possibilities.

When I worry, bad news doesn't bother me so much.
We might call this the Eeyore school of thought, after Winnie-the-Pooh's friend who was constantly pessimistic, gloomy, and depressed. The worrier who goes through life expecting bad things to happen is neither surprised nor knocked down when they do.

Because I always worry, good news feels even better.

This is rather like the person who rationalizes banging their head on the wall because it feels so good when they stop. Worrying feels awful. So when something good happens, the contrast brings even more relief than it might if you were feeling pretty good all along.

In addition to these questionable benefits of chronic anxiety, there is no doubt that some people cling to their worry habits because it allows them to feel purposeful. They identify with their worries, which stimulate them and provide plenty of topics for conversation, adding a dose of drama to what might otherwise be an uninteresting life. Without diving too deep into psychological profiles, there are those who embrace what's called a 'victim consciousness' and thrive on the sympathy and attention that it can provide.

I suppose that it's conceivably possible to believe that these so-called benefits of worry make the awful feelings worthwhile. But when we look at the downside of anxiety, it's hard to imagine that any kind of payoff could make up for the truly ominous side effects of chronic worrying.

There are four main drawbacks to worry and anxiety:

1. *It just feels awful.*

It sucks to be anxious all the time. In fact worry is one of the most unpleasant emotions that we experience as humans. It saps our energy, our strength, and our motivation, and there's a powerlessness that seems to take over, preventing us from taking positive, constructive action. Anxiety comes with its own kind of psychic suffering that can (and does) immobilize you.

Remember Chicken Little? That dim-witted hen who, when an acorn fell on her head, concluded that the sky was falling and proceeded to instill mass panic among the rest of the farmyard animals? It's a cute story, and it's easy to see the folly of jumping to conclusions based on fake news. But too many of us have found ourselves stuck in Chicken Little's head. Like her, I spent way too much of my life convinced that the sky was, indeed, falling. That's how we all feel when we're so trapped in our very real, personal panic. It's impossible to think calmly and rationally. And as imaginary as these demons might be, the power they wield in our psyches makes them impassable roadblocks just the same.

2. *It accomplishes nothing.*

Worry contributes absolutely nothing to your life, to the lives of those around you or to the world. It has never improved any situation or solved any problem. While there are some who might fool themselves into believing that their worry will lead them to a solution to whatever perceived threat is hanging over their heads in the moment, it's never true.

Real problem-solving is a very different mental activity than worrying. Problem-solving requires clear, action-oriented thinking. It rationally assesses the situation, estimates or calculates the relative likelihood of a number of different outcomes, brainstorms and prioritizes potential solutions, weighs the costs and benefits of the different courses of action, then reaches a conclusion and takes action. Worry, on the other hand, simply goes round-and-round in a circle, repeating the same thoughts, over and over again. The curse of anxiety is that it leaves us frozen, oscillating in place, unable to either take decisive action or relax and do nothing.

There is no joy, no purpose, and no resolution in worry. I've never met a single person who honestly enjoys worrying and being anxious. Nor have I met anyone who has found it to be useful in solving a problem or accomplishing a goal. Worry, anxiety, fear, and self-doubt have never left anyone feeling more joyful, healthy, alive, energetic, or better-performing.

3. *It makes you sick.*

It's been more than well documented that stress, worry, and anxiety are injurious to your health. From skin conditions and irritability to high blood pressure, ulcers, and heart attacks, constant worry simply isn't good for you. The Mayo Clinic reports that anxiety can result in restlessness, panic attacks, increased heart rate, hyperventilation, sweating, trembling, feeling weak or tired, trouble concentrating, and gastrointestinal problems. Healthline adds depression, headaches, irritability, heart palpitations, muscle aches, and loss of libido to the list of negative side effects.

Worry can make you simultaneously restless and fatigued. It pumps way too much adrenaline through your veins; makes it difficult to concentrate, work, and sleep; and can make you irritable enough to want to kick the dog.

Whether you're worrying about money, other people's opinions, or that mole on your arm, your body always responds in the same way. It increases your cortisol levels. And that's not good.

Cortisol is produced by your adrenal glands and can be thought of your built-in alarm system. One of its primary roles is to help fuel your body's "fight-or-flight" instinct in a crisis situation. Whenever cortisol is produced, your body goes on high alert, muscles tighten, breathing increases, heart rate goes up, and you're ready to take on the attacking barbarians. If that "code red" status lasts too long, though, some nasty things begin to happen. Too much cortisol compromises your immune system, making you more susceptible to disease. Researchers have also identified relationships between cortisol and diabetes, osteoporosis, and heart disease.

The bottom line is that sustained worry and anxiety can not only make you sick, they can kill you.

4. *It blocks your potential.*

Perhaps the highest price of anxiety, though, is the loss of our innate human potential. Because with every new bogeyman, we dream less, we hesitate more, and the sphere of our infinite potential shrinks. Our potential and performance as human beings is stifled, and we back away from the great things of which our unbridled imaginations are capable. Worries are constraining, restricting, limiting. In the face of them, we believe less, try less, and become less. They cause us to set limits for ourselves before we've even tried. As Zig Ziglar, the great author, salesman, and motivational speaker, said, worry is negative goal-setting and planning for what you don't want.

When you're worrying, you are sending your mental energy somewhere other than where you want to be. The nonstop, low-grade "How-am-I-going-to-pay-the-cable-bill-this-month?," "Why-hasn't-my-friend-like-my-Instagram-post?," "I-think-I'm-supposed-to-worry-more-about-climate-change," "I'm-sure-these-symptoms-mean-I-have-cancer!" kinds of anxiety sap your strength and remove the possibility of greatness.

Then, just for fun, let's add in those self-doubts that are purely the result of our conditioned beliefs. The ones that set limits for us before we've even tried. "I'll never be good at math." "You have to be lucky or criminal to be rich." "I can't get up there and sing karaoke!" This kind of uncontrolled worry-thinking has us giving up before we've even tried.

Remember Hans Christian Andersen's tale "The Emperor's New Clothes?" The dim-witted emperor and townspeople who believed the con men who told them that only the smart people can see the cloth? It's a cautionary tale for those who can't or won't think for themselves. When we allow our imaginations, our psyches, and our inner monologues to be hijacked by fear-mongering headlines and Twitter posts, our wits are also dimmed. And our infinite supply of human potential is stolen. Such a colossal waste!

There are those who seem to want to cling to their worry. They say it makes them feel needed, helpful, or "realistic." But there are far more effective, healthy, and life-affirming ways to show others that you care, stay motivated, or solve problems. Some people simply love the drama. What's life without a battle to be fought and an incoming enemy to be fended off? Some do it so much and revel in it so much that you'd begin to believe that, for them, it's a recreational activity.

But as with any bad habit, the payoffs don't begin to outweigh the drawbacks.

4

THE STRUCTURE OF WORRY

Since the dawn of time there have been things that go bump in the night. For eons we've been afraid of the dark, the boogeyman, and hobgoblins that dwelled only in our minds, yet kept us awake and afraid nonetheless.

Mania or Marketing?

During the last couple of decades, though, we seem to have brought anxiety to a whole new high and perfected the art of allowing perceived, intangible threats to immobilize us. We hear catchphrases such as "Anxiety Epidemic," "Prozac Nation," and the "United States of Xanax" and we watch the rise of what's been dubbed "anxiety consumerism" with a flood of products including fidget spinners, essential oil sprays, and weighted blankets to help us calm down.

The statistics, case studies, and anecdotal evidence are everywhere. The National Institute of Mental Health tells us that 38 percent of girls and 26 percent of boys between the ages of thirteen and seventeen have some type of anxiety disorder. A 2016 study of more than 150,000 students by the Center for Collegiate Mental Health at Pennsylvania State University showed anxiety running well ahead of depression as the most common mental health concern. In 2011 the American College Health Association reported that half of undergraduates felt "overwhelming anxiety." In 2017 that number had risen to 61 percent.

Middle schoolers are suffering from depression, anxiety, and ADHD. Sixth-graders are "freaking out" as they sense the pressure to make top marks in order to be placed in high school honors classes, which would lead to the Advanced Placement classes that are needed to get into college. And parents fight to get their five-year-olds onto the right youth football team because it's a fast track to the NFL and a future of fame and fortune.

Among adults, anxiety is the most prevalent mental health disorder in the US. The Anxiety and Depression Association of America says that 18.1 percent of Americans are affected each year. The National Institute of Mental Health says nearly one-third of Americans will be affected over their lifetimes.

Our online life, of course, is one of the main culprits in this psychic crime. Check your phone before going to sleep, check it again when you get up in the night to pee, and then wake in the morning to the push notification that the Antarctic ice sheets are shrinking. And that doesn't even begin to address the Tweets and Facebook posts that leave us feeling unworthy, left out, and disconnected.

Curiously, while humans have been familiar with fear for millennia, "anxiety" is actually a relative newcomer in our lives. The *Diagnostic and Statistical Manual of Mental Disorders* is the book that the psychiatric profession uses to put a name on what's wrong with you. The term "Generalized Anxiety Disorder" only appeared in the book in 1980.

Even more curious (or perhaps obvious) is that diagnoses of the condition surged after 2001 when GlaxoSmithKline received approval to market Paxil, its antidepressant drug, for the treatment of anxiety. A massive marketing campaign told us to be on the lookout for restlessness, fatigue, irritability, muscle tension, nausea, diarrhea, and sweating, and newscasts reported as many as ten million Americans to be suffering from this "unrecognized" disease.

Maslow's Pyramid

Abraham H. Maslow (1908–1970) was an American psychologist, and it's likely you've heard of some of his work. He's best remembered for theorizing what is known as the 'hierarchy of needs.' This five-tier model of psychological health states that humans have a set of innate needs that we are driven to fulfill. The crux of Maslow's work is that we strive to satisfy those needs in a particular order.

The five tiers of need are frequently illustrated in a pyramid form like this:

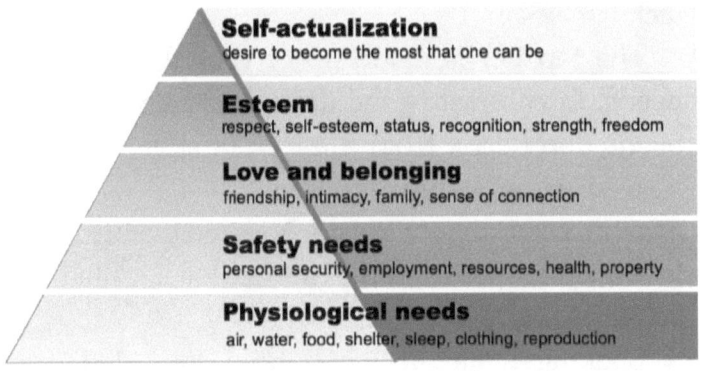

In essence, needs that are lower down in the hierarchy have to be fulfilled before an individual is able to seek out needs that are higher up. In other words, it's hard to think about love and friendship if someone is choking the oxygen out of us, and we aren't overly focused on our social status if we're dying of cancer.

For our purposes in this book, a key to understanding the hierarchy is to see that the five-stage model can be divided into two groups of needs—deficiency needs and growth needs.

The first four levels make up the deficiency needs, which arise from deprivation of some sort. When you are hungry, you're motivated to seek out food; the longer you remain hungry, the more motivated you become. In the same way, the longer you go without friendship or intimacy, the more aware you are of the impact and consequence of its lack.

The top tier is made up of growth, or 'being,' needs. In contrast to the deficiency needs, growth needs don't arise from the lack of something, but instead, from a desire to grow as a person. This growth, according to Maslow, would eventually allow a person to reach the highest level, called self-actualization.

Looking again at the bottom four deficiency needs, they can be divided into two groups. The bottom two can be termed "basic needs," those things that are required for the most basic survival, including food, shelter, safety, and security. The next two can be grouped as "psychological needs," those things we require in order to feel human, such as love, a sense of belonging, and self-esteem.

When we apply Maslow's model to our worries and anxieties, we can see some correlation. We worry about our health, our finances, the security of our homes and neighborhoods. We can easily recognize these anxieties as relating to the two bottom tiers, representing basic needs: Am I going to survive? Will I be alive in the morning? Will I have a place to live and will I be able to buy food?

Even when we have enough to eat and a roof over our heads, the thought (however irrational) that those basic needs might be somehow lost, makes us worry. The point is that everyone just wants to know that things are going to be okay. That they're going to be safe.

We also worry about what others think of us, whether we measure up and fit in. We agonize when our Facebook post isn't liked immediately by every one of our connections. When we take a step back, it's easy to recognize these fears as relating to tiers three and four, representing psychological needs: Is my value recognized by others? Do I have a place of honor in this group? Can I love and be loved? The point, again, is that everyone just wants to know that they're valuable, worthwhile, and respected human beings.

In both these cases, the basic needs and the psychological needs, if there is anything going on out there in the world that we perceive might threaten our fulfillment of those needs (a hurricane forecast, a drop in the Dow Jones Industrial Average, a confusing text from your girlfriend, an unexpected summons to the boss' office . . .) it's far too easy for us to switch into worry-mode.

Reality or Imagination?

Let's make some distinctions among the various threats that seem hell-bent on our destruction. 'Fear,' 'anxiety,' and 'worry' surface when we figure something bad is going to happen. It's useful to think of them as different intensities of the same emotion. In other words, they're all the same thing, just with the dial turned up or down.

Any time your mind perceives that an event is approaching that could end badly for you, one intensity or another of this set of emotions is triggered. In every case, though, the 'event' is something that hasn't yet happened. You're imagining or assuming that it will happen at some future time. But the real truth is that you don't know. This imagined event might or might not actually take place.

- The bus is racing toward you (and you're afraid it's going to flatten you).
- The exams take place at the end of the semester (and you're concerned you won't do well).

- The car payment is due next week (and you're anxious because you don't have the money yet).
- The doctor's appointment is tomorrow at 2:00 (and you're worried you'll get a bad diagnosis).
- My retirement starts in just ten years (and you're nervous your savings won't be sufficient).

None of these events has actually happened. They're all some distance off in the future.

For some events, the likelihood of them coming true is actually pretty high. Hot stoves, hungry tigers, high-voltage wires all fall into the "Oh crap! That bus is about to hit me!" kind of scared, and they're just smart and downright useful survival instincts. Without getting into the fine-grained science that medical degrees and doctoral theses are made of, it will serve our purposes to define fear as a response to this kind of very real danger.

In situations like these, our reactions are always both instantaneous and action-oriented. We're all familiar with the "fight-or-flight" response to a threat. Both of these options involve decisive and immediate action. If the house in on fire, we grab the kids and get the heck out. If the ship is sinking, we make for the lifeboats. If the bully is heading our way on the playground, we either run the other way or stand up and punch him.

Adrenaline pulses through our veins, but it's there for a reason and we make good use of it. Restlessness, fatigue, irritability, muscle tension, and the other symptoms of anxiety we've identified, however, are nowhere to be found. The point is, in a fear-filled emergency, we somehow instinctively know what to do and we don't hesitate to spring into action, fight or flee.

The closer in time the fear-inducing event is, the more we'll respond in that fight-or-flight, immediate and decisive action mode. In fact, when it comes to the fear spectrum, there's something perversely satisfying about a real emergency: it arises, we respond, and it's over. The muscles relax, the adrenaline dissipates, and we clean up the mess.

In contrast, worry and anxiety are responses to threats that are neither immediate nor well defined. Climate change, partisan politics, and your finances in retirement are much more vague, distant, and hard to comprehend than a fast-approaching bus. Sometimes the threats you perceive are only imagined. The right response not only isn't obvious, but there may not be anything we can or should do.

Vague or far-off events like these, though, can trigger that low-grade, chronic anxiety that drains our energy because, while we find ourselves fretting in anticipation of the negative outcome, there seems to be little or nothing we can do about it right now.

Let's take the example of the junior in high school worrying about getting into a good college. College admissions are more than a year in the future and, other than paying attention in class and studying for tests, there is little or nothing that can be done in the moment to address the problem. In fact, it would be erroneous even to label it as a 'problem' at all.

Our poor seventeen-year-old, however, spends hours each day spiraling down into a nightmare of a future in which she isn't accepted into the 'right' school, is ostracized by her friends, disowned by her family, unable to find employment, considered a loathsome loser by any potential mate, and ends up homeless and alone, pushing an abandoned shopping cart and rooting through trash cans for scraps to eat.

Now, it's extremely unlikely that this string of worries is playing out at the level of her conscious thought. In fact, most of our anxiety nightmares hover below our consciousness. But the adrenaline flows and the muscles tense up regardless because your body can't tell the difference between something that's actually happening and something you're simply imagining.

Prove it to yourself
Science has now revealed a tremendous body of evidence in support of the mind-body connection, proving that our thoughts truly do have a direct impact on our bodies and our health. A simple experiment proves this easily:

Sit quietly and close your eyes. Now picture in your mind that you are holding a bright yellow lemon. You feel its texture and you can smell its citrus aroma. In your mind, reach out and pick up the sharp knife that's lying on the table beside you. Lay the lemon on the table, take the knife, and cut the lemon in half. Watch as the lemon juice seeps out onto the surface of the table and smell the intense aroma. Now imagine bringing one of the lemon halves up to your nose and inhaling deeply. Then touch your tongue to the cut surface and taste the bitter lemon juice.

Can you feel your saliva glands activating? There isn't a lemon in sight, but your body responds as if there was one right under your nose. It's unable to tell the difference between reality and what you're simply imagining or what's going on in your subconscious.

The resulting restlessness, fatigue, irritability, and muscle tension—and, unfortunately and increasingly, the popping of Prozac—are very real, however, and of course prevent her from simply paying attention in class, studying for tests, and enjoying being seventeen.

You've may have heard the acronym that defines FEAR as Fantasized Experiences Appearing Real. Absolutely anything that evokes fear, anxiety, or worry is going to, or is imagined as going to, take place in the future. If it has already happened, you're not afraid anymore. You might be angry, injured, broke, or even dead, but you aren't anxious or afraid anymore.

The point of the acronym, however, is that a future event isn't actually real. Right now it exists solely in your imagination. And a great many of the future events over which we agonize never actually come to pass.

We writhe in mental agony over the diagnosis we're convinced we will get, the lover we're sure is having an affair, the exam we're terrified we'll fail, or the nut-job with a gun we're sure is walking through the mall, yet these events virtually never materialize.

Even though these 'events' exist purely in our imagined future, we've taught ourselves to fear them as if they were both very real and very immediate. Perhaps it's time we unlearned that lesson.

5

IT'S JUST A HABIT
AND HABITS CAN BE REPLACED

We've been in the laboratory for a while now, studying and analyzing our test subject—worry and anxiety. We've learned a few important things already that are going to make a big difference in your ability to opt out of them. So far, we've learned:

- The world around us is working hard to make worriers out of us all. Between 24/7 news, social media, and our own tendency to love drama, we're led to believe that the circumstances, people, and events around us are conspiring to end life as we know it.
- While scary news grabs the headlines, there are actually far more good things going on than bad. It's just that hardly anyone is paying attention to that side of the news.

- Our brains are designed with a 'negativity bias.' While it was originally designed to keep us from being some predator's meal, today it's alerting us to questionable Facebook posts.
- Throughout our lives we've been trained and conditioned to be anxious. Our parents, teachers, coaches, and the entire world around us frets, so it must be the thing to do. Who, ever, questions the wisdom of worrying?
- While there might be those who would try to convince you of the marginal and highly suspect advantages of worrying, the downsides can be toxic to the point of endangering our health and even our lives.
- Anxiety is a response to a perception that we're about to be deprived of one or more of our fundamental needs, which will threaten either our existence or our ability to belong.
- If the threat is real, we instinctively know what to do. Far more often, though, the danger exists only in our imaginations.
- Worrying feels awful and never, ever improves the situation.

In all that we've learned about anxiety, there isn't a single thing that indicates that it's a fact of life, that it's necessary for survival, or that it adds to your quality of life. The only thing we've discovered is that we have this 'negativity bias' that, like your appendix, stopped serving a useful function long ago. And note that it's merely a 'bias,' meaning that it's a tendency or an inclination, not a hard-wired, must-do reflex. Our well-established ability to think rationally can easily override it.

The only conclusion we can reasonably reach is that worrying is something we're choosing to do. Not consciously perhaps, but choosing nonetheless. That our minds always and immediately fly to the negative, even to the worst possible outcome, is not somehow programmed into our synapses. Worry and anxiety are choices that we make.

The problem, though, is that we've been choosing worry and anxiety so consistently and for so long that it's become a habit. And this worry habit has been reinforced so strongly and has become so familiar that it now appears to be our natural state. Because worry is such an ingrained habit, we never give any thought to whether or not it's wise or useful.

We all have habits of one sort or another. Many are extremely useful. You walk into the house at the end of the day and, without even thinking, toss your car keys into the dish that sits on the table by the door. The act is so automatic and unconscious that you're likely not even aware that you're doing it. It's a handy thing, though, because tomorrow morning you won't have to spend any time looking for your keys. They're right where they're supposed to be because your ingrained habit put them there. Habits can relieve us of the need to repeatedly solve the same problem or perform the same action. They save our brainpower for things that are more important or interesting.

Not all habits, though, are beneficial. Biting your nails, picking up your phone to check emails or Facebook posts, watching too much TV . . . there is a long list of habitual behaviors that we'd all be better off without. Some, unfortunately, become addictions that have an additional chemical or physiological challenge when it comes time to break them.

Worrying is one of our most common bad habits. Like any habit, the behavior has been going on so long and has become so ingrained and unconscious, we never give any thought to whether or not it's wise or useful. As we've seen, there is nothing the least bit rational or useful about worry, and it's never a beneficial or intelligent response. It's just that we've been doing it so long that, when a negative situation arises or appears to arise, it seems to be the obvious and only thing to do. It's a habitual way of thinking that you've developed, practiced, and perfected over many years.

We've learned that most of our anxieties and

worries were implanted from a very young age. It could have been that your parents worried about money and reminded you frequently that money doesn't grow on trees. Maybe it was so-called friends in middle school who left you anxious about your appearance when they teased you about some not-yet-gone baby fat. Or the gym coach who smirked at your athletic attempts and left you feeling that you never measure up. Or the dire TV news anchor who said, "Good evening" and then proceeded to tell you why there wasn't the least thing 'good' about it.

Regardless of how your anxieties began and who might be convenient to blame, they're yours to suffer now.

Or to vanquish.

And believe me, you *can* conquer them. Because worry and anxiety are mental habits it's entirely possible to replace them with different habits. In other words, our anxieties and worries are entirely self-imposed and come with an 'off' switch.

Ceaseless, Pointless Mentation

Mentation is, essentially, mental activity or the act of thinking, and we do it all the time. Experts can't seem to agree how many discrete thoughts we have every day, but estimates range from 20,000 to 70,000. Rest assured, it's a lot. For chronic worriers, many, if not most, of those thoughts are problem-focused.

Many habitual worriers like to claim that their anxiety helps them solve the problems they believe they're facing. But problem-solving is a very different activity than worrying. It's rational, it's action-oriented, and it makes progress. When you're worrying, your mentation takes on a very different tone. It's very easy to tell the difference for yourself.

If your thinking is primarily worry-focused, you'll find that, throughout the day, you're regurgitating the same mental contents of yesterday. Yesterday's thoughts were essentially the same as those of last week, last month, and even a year ago. Your thinking goes round-and-round in circles and always ends up back where you began, concerned about money, health, relationships, or the low-pressure zone that's forming in the eastern Atlantic. Most telling, though, is that your thoughts don't feel good. But no matter how drained, down, and crappy the thoughts make you feel, you're simply unable to stop them from cycling around, over and over again.

Mentation that's aimed at problem-solving, in contrast, makes you feel good. It feels like you're moving forward towards a solution. The process might be tough and challenging, but it's also productive. You weigh options, test ideas, and make choices. As with worry, you might also feel drained after a problem-solving session, but you additionally feel like you've accomplished something useful. That the effort was worthwhile. Instead of circling back to the same place you were yesterday, you can see the progress that you've made and it feels satisfying.

One of the keys to unsubscribing from anxiety, which we'll talk about in detail in Part 2, is learning to pay attention to and become more aware of the nature of our thoughts. By learning to distinguish between a good old-fashioned worry-fest and productive, progressive, problem-solving, we can take the first steps to controlling and eventually overcoming the pointless and debilitating habit of worrying.

Are Your Thoughts Trustworthy?

One of the characteristics of worrying is how easily and frequently we spin off, spiraling down through layers and layers of ever-increasing terrors. Here's how it works:

> *We hear a news item about the Dow Jones falling five hundred points today. Some pundit then goes on to tell us how the economy is overdue for a major correction and this is likely just the beginning. They dig up and recycle stories from 1929, 1987, 2008, and every*

other time the stock exchange has taken a dive. "Experts" are interviewed about what this means to the average investor and how this is likely to hit the 'regular Joe's' 401(k) accounts, mutual funds, and retirement savings.

This doom and gloom has you in a panic about your own investments, and you begin to imagine your savings being flushed down one gigantic toilet bowl. Your throat tightens and your pulse rate goes up as you think about having to work three jobs for the next ten years to recover these losses. No, wait, you're too old! It will be impossible to recover them! Now you're imagining retirement in a rusty old single-wide trailer, parked outside some nowhere town as you wander the streets looking for bottles and cans to turn in for a few bucks at the recycling center while hoping to scrounge enough for the cans of cat food that will have to serve as your dinner.

Twenty-four hours later, you hear another news item that the Dow recovered yesterday's losses and went on to a record close.

So much for the self-administered nightmare.

As rational and intelligent human beings, we put a great deal of stock and faith in our ability to think.

We register informational input, we process it, we reach conclusions, and we make decisions.

But what if our thoughts aren't always trustworthy? What if they aren't as reliable as we like to think they are? The fact is, there are limits to rationale and reason. And even when those limits are very high, there are also very real obstacles to them functioning properly and reliably.

Many things affect our ability to think accurately and reliably. Have you ever had a few glasses of wine and found yourself saying or doing things that, in the clear light of the next morning, might not have been so wise? Have you ever been overcome with emotion—perhaps anger, jealousy, or even joy—and found yourself entertaining thoughts or making judgments, either negative or positive, that later seemed a little unreasonable?

Aside from true cognitive impairment brought on by disease or aging, there are many things in daily life that can and do impair our ability to think clearly. Fear, anxiety, and worry are high on the list. We learned earlier that anxiety can make it hard to concentrate, which is one of our important cognitive functions. Studies have also shown that anxiety can affect perception, attention, learning, and executive functions, which are the processes that have to do with mental control and self-regulation.

Conclusions we reach and decisions we make in

the midst of anxiety or worry are at high risk of being unreliable. And yet, caught up in the whirlwind of worry, they seem logical, inevitable, and terrifying. We accept those conclusions and decisions as true and then are stuck living a life that is encumbered and limited by these erroneous beliefs.

All for the sake of a simple habit that we mistakenly assume is a fact of life. A habit that is easily replaced. A habit that serves no one.

6

BRINGING IT ON

While the world around us seems to be cheering on our worry habit, there are a couple of factors that we ourselves bring to the table that also reinforce the practice. The first has to do with our physiology, the other with the world of physics.

Once we understand how these factors operate and affect us, we can easily begin to turn them to our advantage in our efforts to opt out of worry and anxiety.

Make Friends with Your RAS

According to the *Encyclopedia of Neuroscience*, the Reticular Activating System (RAS) is a piece of your brain that is "located in the mesopons, which interacts with descending reticulospinal and ascending hypothalamic, basal forebrain, and thalamocortical systems," a definition that doesn't help us in the least. Instead, let's call it is a bundle of nerves in your brainstem. Its function is to automatically filter out unnecessary information so the important stuff can get our attention.

What's the 'important stuff'? It's the stuff we think about most. Your RAS is why you can be standing in a noisy room and yet clearly hear when someone across the room says your name. It's the thing that lets you be in a deep sleep while the TV is still on, but wake up instantly when your baby starts to cry in the next room. It's why, when you start thinking that a red sports car might be a nice thing to own, you start suddenly seeing them everywhere.

It's not that the red sports cars weren't there before, it's just that your RAS takes what you focus on and creates a filter for it. It then uses the data that your five senses are constantly supplying, filters through it all, and presents your conscious brain with only those things that you've told it are important. Your RAS takes your predominant thoughts—whether you find those thoughts to be pleasant and useful or not—and assumes they represent what is most important to you. And it goes looking for images, thoughts, and circumstances that match.

Here's a quick experiment that you can try. Close your eyes for a moment and think about the color blue. Picture it, imagine it, put the word and the image of 'blue' solidly in your mind. Now open your eyes and look around the room. See how many blue things jump out at you? Even the tiniest ones become almost glaring in your vision. Now think about yellow and notice all the stuff that you didn't see when you were thinking about blue.

Your RAS is like the search function on your computer but massively more powerful. Not only will it seek out colors, objects, and images that we think about, it's also programmed by what we focus on and what we identify with. For example, if you're a mechanic, you drive down the street and notice all the cars that are making a funny noise, have faint blue smoke coming from the exhaust pipe, or have a ding in the door. If you're on the police force, you notice all the suspicious-looking people on the street.

None of this happens at your level of consciousness. It's all going on in the background, but you get to consciously register the results. As the mechanic, it would be very easy for you to start believing that the majority of cars on the road need repairs of one sort or another.

Here's where things get really interesting for our anxiety investigation: While the RAS spends its time looking for things and circumstances that match your thoughts, it also seeks information, people, news items, and any other evidence it can find that validate your beliefs.

Your thoughts and beliefs provide the parameters, and the RAS finds things in the world that confirm them. If you believe and spend time worrying that your neighborhood isn't safe, you'll have a hard time seeing anything except shady characters and run-down properties. If your neighbor, on the other hand, believes that your section of town is delightful, they'll notice nothing but the bright flowers, the young family moving in, and the new streetlights. Should you point out the rusty old car that's up on blocks in a front yard, they likely won't have noticed it before and simply interpret it as a harmless anomaly.

The point is, when you are absorbed with your fears, anxieties, and worries, your RAS, in its effort to match your thoughts, goes looking for evidence that supports those thoughts. When your thoughts are constantly bolstered, you've created a self-reinforcing belief system and a set of self-fulfilling prophecies. In other words, your RAS will confirm your own worst fears.

And it gets even more fun!

In the process of filtering what you see and hear to match what you believe, the RAS will also influence your actions. If you are afraid that you'll never find a good relationship partner, you'll discover yourself dating a string of losers. If you think that money is hard to come by, you will prove yourself correct.

You've likely heard of the concept of self-sabotage—those behaviors, frequently subconscious, that undermine and interfere with our stated goals. Procrastination, comfort eating, and overspending are common examples. You may be chronically worried about your finances in retirement, but every month you have things that, for one reason or another, just have to be paid for with funds that would otherwise be saved. These behaviors can come from a variety of sources, self-limiting beliefs, childhood training, or low self-esteem to name a few. But, unless one is suffering from a true mental illness, it's possible to retrain your RAS and eliminate the unwanted behaviors.

Your RAS leads you to focus on and see those things you think about most. Now, you might protest that you don't think about poverty, you constantly think about how to get more money. You don't think about getting sick and landing in the hospital, you want so very much to be healthy and well. And here's where things get subtle. There are two sides to every thought—the aspect of it that you want, and the aspect of it that you want to avoid.

You don't want to struggle with finances	You do want to enjoy abundance
You don't want to be sick	You do want to be healthy
You don't want to be lonely	You do want to have love in your life

When we really examine and analyze those things we spend most of our time worrying about, we discover that our minds are dwelling on what we don't want.

- I'm worried about not being able to make the mortgage payment
- I'm worried that my boyfriend will fall out of love with me
- I'm worried that this mole on my arm will become cancerous

And our RAS, ever eager to do its job, shows us more and more of what we don't want. Which makes us even more convinced that the bad thing is going to happen, which makes the RAS work even harder to go out and find it in the world, which makes us . . .

You get the picture.

In sharp contrast, when you begin to focus on what is going well, your RAS finds more things that are going well, presents solutions to your current problems, and things get better and better. We're going to examine this in more detail in Part 3.

Tenth Grade Physics Class

If you were paying attention in tenth-grade physics, you may remember a little experiment with tuning forks. If you recall, a tuning fork is a little metal thingy that looks like a two-pronged fork, formed from a U-shaped bar of metal. When you strike it, it begins to vibrate, emitting a pure and specific musical tone that is unique to the size and shape of the fork. A fork that is tuned to sound the note of A, which is equal to 440 hertz, can only ever emit an A.

The experiment required two tuning forks, both tuned to the same note. When the science teacher struck one of them and it began to vibrate, the other fork, located some distance away, would start to vibrate and emit its note too. The experiment is used to demonstrate a phenomenon called sympathetic vibration or resonance. When the first fork is struck, its vibration sends energy waves toward the second fork. Because it's tuned to the same vibrational frequency, the energy waves resonate with the second fork and it begins to resonate as well. This is also the trick behind the opera singer who can shatter a wine glass with her voice.

Now let's move on to some graduate-degree physics.

Beginning in the late 1800s and famously continuing with Albert Einstein, scientists have been learning about quantum physics, the structure and behavior of the tiniest particles in the universe. Among the discoveries are two remarkable notions.

The first is that the smaller and smaller the particles get, the less and less 'stuff' is actually there. In other words, scientists have discovered that what we see, touch, and think of as 'matter,' the hard stuff of the world, is, at its most fundamental level, nothing but energy. When we look at the tiniest 'things' through the most powerful microscopes, we discover there are no 'things' at all, just vibrating energy.

The second remarkable discovery is that, as scientists conduct experiments with these most minute particles, the results of those experiments actually depend on their expectations. Odd as it may seem, if a researcher expects one result, she gets it. If she expects something different, she gets that. The researcher's thoughts and intentions truly do influence the experimental outcome.

A conclusion that researchers are reaching is

that, like the vibrations of the tuning fork, our thoughts are actually a form of vibrational energy that go out and resonate with other thoughts. Additionally, since everything in the universe is also nothing but vibrating energy, our thoughts also resonate with things that match their resonance. This is the basis of what you've likely heard of as the law of attraction.

This concept states that, because of their vibrational nature, your thoughts have the power to attract similar thoughts and even events and circumstances that match your thoughts. In other words, if you spend all your time thinking that bad things are going to happen to you, you're creating a self-fulfilling prophecy.

It's been said that worry is using your mental energy to create a future that you don't want. If you spend an inordinate amount of time worrying—about money, about love, about your health—it's extremely likely that, between your RAS and the law of attraction, your worry is actually bringing those fears into your life. Rather than helping you find solutions, anxiety is making the problem worse.

Let's go back to something we discussed earlier with regard to our Reticular Activating System, which is that there are two sides to every anxious thought—the aspect of it that you want and that which you don't want.

- I *do* want to be fit and healthy.
- I *don't* want to be weak and sick.

While your conscious self might be thinking about the "I *do* . . ." or the "I *don't* . . ." and assuming that those are the significant parts of those statements, your subconscious, your RAS, and the law of attraction focus on the "fit and healthy" or the "weak and sick" sections of those thoughts.

Try it for yourself: Close your eyes and focus on the thought, "I *don't* want to be weak and sick." Notice the subtle feelings that you evoke as you think about it. They're likely feelings of fear and aversion, and you can't help having images of lethargy, doctor visits, and low energy.

Now close your eyes again and focus on the thought, "I *do* want to be fit and healthy." Again, notice how different this thought feels than the previous one. It feels uplifting, happy, lighthearted, and even joyous. The images in your mind are about healthy eating, an active lifestyle, and high energy.

Because the feelings you experience are the actual vibrations that your thoughts have generated, both the RAS and the law of attraction resonate far more intensely to the feelings than they do to the conscious thoughts. And both will work to bring you closer to the thing that you spend most of your time and mental energy focusing on.

The beauty of both is also that, once we've learned how they work, we can use them to our advantage. Rather than using your worry and anxiety to create a future that you don't want, create the future that you *do* want?

7

YOU *CAN* STOP WORRYING

By now we've spent a lot of time together, learning a tremendous amount about anxiety, fear, and worry. We've learned some of their origins, how people (including those closest to you) love to propagate them, how they affect your cognitive functions, and the negative outcomes of allowing them to dominate your mind.

In all this study, though, there hasn't been a single piece of evidence that proves or even suggests that anxiety and worry are something you have no choice about. You may have been born with brown eyes and curly hair, but short of wearing dark glasses and a hat, you're pretty much stuck with them. But you weren't born worrying. That's something you picked up along the way and are fully capable of putting back down.

We noted earlier that there's a general belief that

you were born with two and only two fears—the fear of loud noises and the fear of falling. Remember your carefree days as a child? You didn't worry about a thing until your parents, teachers, coaches, and the world around you convinced you that you should. From that point on, every worry, anxious moment, or fear that you've experienced has been learned, adopted, or conditioned from your experiences through the years.

It might be tempting to say that children are naïve and don't understand the threats that the 'real world' imposes. But how often do we wish or seek guidance to be more childlike again? Children don't spend time thinking about all the terrible things that might happen. They live in the moment, take delight and joy in the smallest things, and deal with life as it comes along.

Over the years you've become extremely good at dealing with life as it comes along—the proof is that, after all these years, you're still alive. You have successfully dealt with every single threat or obstacle that the world has thrown at you. There isn't a single thing that has defeated you.

You might object and say that you've taken your share of bumps and bruises, nasty collisions even. And still, here you are today—alive, breathing, thinking, and wanting to become an even greater version of yourself by learning how to abandon this silly habit of worry. That's proof enough of your ability to survive, prosper, grow, and be victorious.

Take a moment to pat yourself on the back! When you think about all the threats, risks, hazards, perils, and pressures that you've laid awake nights worrying about, not a single one has taken you down. In spite of all the mental and emotional energy you've invested in anxiety over all the terrible tragedies that you were concerned might befall you, there hasn't been one that won. Sure, you may have been down on the mat occasionally. You may even have been close to throwing in the towel. But you didn't. You're still here, still reaching for the next prize.

That's worth taking a moment—or an entire week!—to celebrate!

Now think about this: Since you've managed to get this far and achieve this much, all the while you were carrying this ridiculous, unneeded, and extremely heavy burden of worry and anxiety, imagine how far you can go, the miracles you can achieve, and the heights you can reach if you *weren't* loaded down with worry! It staggers the imagination!

I've never met a single person who enjoys worrying and being anxious. Nor have I met anyone who has found it to be useful in solving a problem or accomplishing a goal. In fact, absolutely no one feels more joyful, healthy, alive, energetic, and better-performing as a result of worry or anxiety.

Worry and anxiety are mental habits. They result from years and years of being trained, conditioned, and coached to fret about what might be coming. But to remain in worry mode, to allow anxiety to dominate your thoughts, is to give your power away to a future that is unlikely to even materialize. It's to let others dictate who you should be, what you should do, how you should think, and how you should live your life.

There is no joy in worry—worry contributes absolutely nothing to your life or to the world. So let's just stop it. Let's do something else, something more constructive instead.

Breaking Habits

Where do we go from here?

Recall that, with the exception of meaningless platitudes such as "Don't worry!", no one discouraged you from worrying or taught you any different, more useful responses to perceived threats, so your worrying grew to be an automatic habit. Not a pleasant or useful one, but a habit nonetheless. And that's the most encouraging thing about this whole anxiety business. It's completely optional.

Like any habit, you can decide to break it.

UNSUBSCRIBE FROM ANXIETY

Prove it to yourself
Let's look at a small, insignificant habit that you have in order to get a glimpse at what it might take to break a habit.

Set the book down for a moment and fold your hands in the familiar gesture that you've done all your life. Some fold their hands like this during prayer, others simply find it a comfortable position. The meaning is irrelevant — simply interlock your fingers and thumbs with your palms facing together like this.

Once you have your hands folded, notice how familiar and comfortable it feels. Your fingers lace together as they have thousands of times before and you could sit

relaxed like this for a long time.

Now look down and notice which of your thumbs is on the top. For some it might be the right, for others the left. My right thumb always lands on top but there is absolutely no significance to either.

Now unlink your fingers and shift them all down by just one. In other words, if your right thumb and right forefinger were on top at first, shift them down so that the left thumb and left forefinger are at the top of your little finger pile.

How does it feel to cross your fingers in a different way than usual? Does it feel uncomfortable, as if something's wrong and out of place? Things just aren't right, and you're anxious to move them back to their more comfortable, familiar arrangement.

If you really examine your hands and your fingers, you'll discover that, physiologically and anatomically, there is nothing whatsoever that would dictate how you fold your hands. Yet because you've always been doing it the same way—right on top or left on top—you've developed and become extremely comfortable in that habitual behavior. To alter the habit feels uncomfortable, and we want to get back to the familiar as quickly as possible.

If, for the next several weeks, however, every time you were to fold your hands you consciously did it in the new, unfamiliar arrangement, you'd notice two things. First, you would have to work at it and remind yourself regularly to change things up. It would feel like an effort, and you'd be wondering why you should bother. Second, after a couple of weeks, the new arrangement would begin to feel much more familiar and comfortable and would eventually begin to be your new, automatic habit.

Now there's no particular benefit to be gained by training yourself to fold your hands in a different arrangement than you always have. But the lesson is apt—you can, with a little effort, but not nearly as much as you might think, replace any habit you choose with a different one, also of your choosing. A new habit that serves you better and is more productive and more beneficial to you. You're beginning to take control of your mind instead of it controlling you.

What Would You Become?

"I wished to live deliberately . . . and not, when I came to die, discover that I had not lived."
—Henry David Thoreau

There's a cute little movie from 2006 starring Queen Latifah called *Last Holiday* in which she plays a shy, unassuming store clerk. She longs to be a professional chef and records her dreams of a better life in a journal labeled "Possibilities." But rather than stepping up to her possibilities, she carefully saves her money for that rainy day, never colors outside the lines, and lives a drab, unfulfilling life. When she's diagnosed with a fatal illness and given just a few weeks to live, she liquidates her savings and embarks on her dream vacation.

As she's contemplating the dream life that never materialized, she reflects, *"Next time... we will laugh more, we'll love more; we just won't be so afraid."*

What, over your life, or even over the last few years, have you failed to try because of fear or anxiety?

What would you try in the future if you were free of it? Think, for a moment, about how life would feel if you were absolutely free of worry and anxiety. What would you do if you weren't the least bit afraid to fail, succeed, change, be judged, look foolish, say 'no,' or try something completely different? If you were, as Thoreau says, "living deliberately," what would be different in your life than it is today?

We all have a list of things we'd love to do, "If only I weren't afraid of . . ." "If only I weren't afraid to . . ." That's the worst thing about anxiety and worry—they hold us back from living the lives we dream about. They put the brakes on our potential and limit what we can become.

One college professor asked his students to list

the things they'd do if only they weren't afraid. Here's the list they compiled.

If I weren't afraid, I would:

1. Go back to being the person I used to be
2. Stop giving in to the demons in my head
3. Try out for a singing show
4. Dye my hair purple
5. Love myself 100 percent
6. Stop worrying about letting the people I love down and being a total failure at life
7. Ask my girlfriend to marry me
8. Not think twice about the choices I make that I know deep down are right
9. Freely express my thoughts and opinions without worrying about what others may think
10. Drop out and work on the start-up I've always dreamed about
11. Be a high school history or English teacher
12. Coach football, baseball, or basketball
13. Tell handsome guys I thought they were handsome
14. Go without makeup sometimes
15. Kiss all the girls I can
16. Take as many AP classes as possible without thinking of failing
17. Tell the boy that I like how I actually feel about him

18. Tell my fake friends how I really feel about them
19. Go to any college that I got into without fear of the loans I would take out
20. Do what I *actually* want to do when I grow up without the fear of thinking I won't cut it
21. Stop believing that I'm disappointing my parents
22. Stop being afraid of failing at life
23. Ride roller coasters and do more things that give you an adrenaline rush
24. Speak about my religious beliefs to everyone
25. Skydive
26. Stand up for myself
27. Say "no" more often
28. Wear whatever I want
29. Become a public speaker
30. Bring awareness to the problems the world faces today
31. Sleep with the lights off at night
32. Stand up to people when they are hurting me emotionally
33. Voice my opinion and not care what other people think
34. Just up and go
35. Make more conversation with people I don't know
36. Become a touring musician
37. Write and publish a book

38. Attend a meditation retreat
39. Travel abroad . . . by myself
40. Earn a doctoral degree

Now, what's on that list of yours?

In this section I've been showing you why it's such a good idea to let go of your fear of fear. In the next section I'm going to show you *how* to grant yourself the permission and power to leave fear, anxiety, and worry behind. I'm going to show you how to choose joy and find the mental freedom to pursue your limitless potential. I'm going to give you the inspiration and resources to overcome fear and anxiety and unleash the infinite greatness that is your birthright regardless of your origins, upbringing, education, intelligence, or current circumstances.

I'm going to help you unleash your built-in fear-fighter.

Part 2—Opting Out of Worry

In this part you're going to learn the art of leaving anxiety and worry behind. You're going to discover that anxiety has an "off" switch and that it's entirely possible for you to take control of your fears and have them leave you. It will be as if you've grown tired of a particular piece of furniture in your home. It's outlasted its usefulness, and it's time to be rid of it and replace it with something that's new, fresh, and pleasing.

You'll discover that your anxiety will have no more hold over you than that old piece of worn-out furniture. You'll find that it's just as easy to rid yourself of the worry as it is to throw out that ratty old sofa.

8

TAKING 100 PERCENT RESPONSIBILITY

The first step to freeing yourself from worry and anxiety is to take 100 percent responsibility for absolutely everything that happens to you and in your life. This principle is fundamental to ridding yourself of worry and creating a joyful life and must be tackled first. It is essential to master responsibility first because everything that follows is based on and requiring of this principle being solidly in place.

In Part 1 we discovered that worry and anxiety are thoughts that we entertain within our minds. The things that cause us to have these thoughts are always circumstances, events, people, etc. that are outside and external to our minds. The economy is struggling, terrorism is on the rise, weather patterns are changing for the worse, this mole on my arm seems to be getting bigger, my mother is always judging me.

Because the things we worry and fret about are

always out there in the physical world, external to our minds, we easily and conveniently develop the thinking habit that "If only those circumstances would change, I wouldn't have to worry so much." So we complain about those circumstances and blame those we feel are or ought to be responsible for them.

- "If the banks weren't so greedy, the economy would not be hit by these huge drops."
- "The fault lies with the (Republicans) (Democrats)! If they weren't so obstructionist, things could get done in Washington!"
- "If big industry would take a more environmentally friendly approach and not be so focused on their bottom lines, we wouldn't be seeing these climate change effects."
- "Why can't my mother understand that I want to live my life by my own rules, not hers?"

We spend an inordinate amount of time finding the culprits, passing judgment and placing blame on them for the circumstances in which we find ourselves. And nothing changes. As long as we invest our time, our energy, and our emotions in blaming and complaining about how things are, we will never be able to stop worrying and create the lives we want to live.

As soon as you place the blame for your circumstances on someone else, you surrender all your power. As long as you believe that someone else's behavior is responsible for your situation and emotional state, you have handed all your ability to change things over to them. Because unless and until they decide to change the way they're acting, your situation will remain exactly the same.

Now, admittedly, it could very well be that someone else's actions resulted in your circumstances. Your company was acquired and you were downsized. Your girlfriend fell out of love with you and left. The city passed a new ordinance and you can no longer keep chickens in your backyard. Expecting them to or insisting that they change the way they behave in order to please you, though, is a fool's game. It's simply not going to happen.

As we noted previously, the world is, in fact, conspiring to make you anxious, and it's both tempting and easy to blame CNN, Facebook, the politicians, or your mother for whatever is happening around you. But it does you no good at all. Because, at the end of the day, it's you who is doing the worrying, you who is losing sleep, and you who is suffering the high blood pressure. Since none of the rest of them are stepping up to bring an end to your anxiety, if it's going to happen, it's up to you.

Looking for others to provide the solutions to

your problems distracts you and wastes your time and energy. It's far more effective to look for the solutions inside yourself. The anxiety-producing event has happened or is happening. By assuming 100 percent responsibility for what happens next, you take 100 percent of the power to resolve the problem for yourself.

Previously we talked about how we can attract our conditions and circumstances to ourselves through the thoughts we think, the images we hold in our minds, and the behaviors we exhibit in the world. As we discussed, we create our experiences, our success, the quality of our relationships, and our health by our thoughts and beliefs, the visual images, both actual and mental, that we focus on, the emotions they create, and our actions. And we each have full and complete control over our thoughts and beliefs, the visual images on which we choose to focus, and our actions.

That last point is worth repeating, with emphasis: *We each have full and complete control over our thoughts and beliefs, the visual images on which we choose to focus, and our actions.*

No one can tell you what to think, what to imagine, or what to do. You always have a choice. Admittedly, sometimes the choice is between two bad options, but the fact is, you always have the choice. And in that fact lies your power.

There is a simple formula that can help you understand and embrace this idea of taking 100 percent responsibility for whatever is happening in your life:

$$E + R = O$$
Event + Response = Outcome

An event takes place—you watch a TV news report about a mugging in your neighborhood, you hear that the company you work for is being sold, you realize that final exams are in two weeks. What happens next is entirely within your power to control. If you don't like the outcomes you've been getting up until now, which include sleepless nights and high blood pressure, you have two choices:

1. You can blame the event (E), for your circumstances and your anxiety.

This choice, however, leaves you powerless. The ability to change your outcomes is controlled by others—the economy, the weather, your spouse, your boss, your parents, the alignment of the stars, if you want. And not one of them is offering to change things to please you.

2. You can change your response (R) to the event (E) until you get the outcome (O) you want.

It's helpful to define "events" as "the way things

are." In other words, the "event" is the fact that your mother is very judgmental of you, your colleague is difficult to work with, the economy is going in the tank, or you have a doctor's appointment to look at that suspicious mole on your back.

Thousands, if not millions of people have faced the same circumstances (events) that you are now facing. Some percentage of them decided that they were powerless and destined to suffer whatever dire consequences this oncoming menace would dish out. They continued to suffer the agony of anxiety. But many others chose to take the power into their own hands. They changed their thinking, they changed their communication, they changed the pictures they held in their heads. And they succeeded.

Let's take a look at the examples of "events" I mentioned earlier and see how the two choices might play out.

You've just seen a TV news report about a mugging in your neighborhood.

Choice #1: You phone your like-minded neighbor and spend an hour commiserating about how much things have gone downhill in the last few years. During the call the two of you cite four other instances in which bad things have happened or signs that the neighborhood is deteriorating. You pour yourself a stiff drink in order to calm your nerves and spend a restless night listening for noises that you're convinced are someone trying to break in.

Choice #2: You remind yourself that the news station gets higher ratings when they highlight 'high drama' stories and switch the TV to a channel with an uplifting movie or a concert. You resolve to do some of your own research on local crime statistics to determine for yourself whether this is a trend or an anomaly and you make a donation to the re-election campaign for the candidate you believe is committed to bringing more diversity and new businesses to the neighborhood. Then you climb into bed and sleep like a baby.

You hear that the company you work for is being sold.
Choice #1: You instantly begin to tell yourself stories about how old you are, how out-of-date your qualifications are, and how hard it is for someone your age to start over. You recall seeing your boss with some people you didn't recognize in a confidential meeting last week and convince yourself that it was new management going over the keep-or-don't-keep employee list. You go home, have too many beers at dinner, and spend the night with an upset stomach and a headache.

Choice #2: You schedule a meeting for tomorrow

afternoon with your boss and ask her to tell you, honestly, what she can about what's going on so that you can best prepare for the change. You recall all the news stories you've been reading lately about why fifty-plus can be the best age to start a business. You have an open conversation with your spouse and let them know that you're kinda scared and kinda excited at the same time and you're going to need their support through this. Then you decide to get serious about launching that online course about building wooden boats that you've been promising to do for years.

You realize that final exams are in two weeks.

Choice #1: You're filled with regret about the classes you skipped, the tutorials you slept through, and the books you haven't yet read. You go into panic mode and start cramming for eighteen hours a day, living on caffeine and donuts. The whole time you're trying to study, you can't stop thinking about how hard it will be to pay off your student loan after you fail this semester and they ask you to leave the school since no one hires failures.

Choice #2: You take a couple of hours to put together a study schedule that includes time for rest and exercise as well as nutritional eating. You head into the process systematically, starting with the areas you know are your weakest and leaving your strong subjects till the end. You regularly remind yourself that you're a smart person who enjoys challenges and you work with a study partner who is calm and collected. You admit that there is probably more that you could have done through the year but you're going to do the best you can.

There are times when none of the choices you have are appealing. For example, I mentioned earlier how, in the early days of the great recession, I was unable to make the mortgage payments on a house that I was trying to sell. The bank foreclosed and I went through about five years of rebuilding my credit rating.

At the time, though, I had some choices, none of which were good. I needed money and had exhausted every legitimate resource I could think of. So my remaining choices included:

- Getting drunk, complaining about my bad luck or bad treatment and worrying about what was going to happen
- Robbing a bank
- Defrauding or conning someone
- Defaulting on my mortgage

In this case I chose the "least-worst" option and settled in to work my way back out of the hole in which I found myself. When the choices you're left with in any situation aren't to your liking, it's an opportunity to assess how you got there, what to do next, and how to avoid the situation in the future. All of which is much more productive than looking for someone or some circumstance to blame. And all of which is entirely within your control.

Even when all your choices are bad, the last choice you always have is your attitude. You may have heard of Viktor Frankl. He was a Jewish psychiatrist in Austria in the years leading up to World War II. As with millions of his faith, he ended up in a concentration camp in the most horrendous conditions possible with people dying all around him. Frankl, however, made a decision. He decided that no one would own his spirit, and he chose to find meaning and purpose. He discovered that those people who chose hope survived longer and, following the war, he wrote a book about his experiences that has become a classic: *Man's Search for Meaning*.

The choices in front of you may not be great, and choosing A over B may land you in water that is only slightly less hot. Make the best choice you can under the circumstances, then own that choice! And maybe that choice is to change your attitude about the circumstances. You always have a choice about your attitude. Leave your job or change your mind about your job. Leave your marriage or change your mind about your marriage.

Let's face it—life occasionally hands you a sour one. But the more you fight against "what is," the harder you push against it, the more "what is" will push back. The more you protest that it's not fair or right, the more you'll discover that "what is" is bigger and stronger than you. The more you worry, the higher your blood pressure while you make no progress.

When you relax and accept "what is" for what it is, though, you regain the power to choose your response and influence your outcomes to those that are much better suited to your preferences.

The "event" (E) is out of your control. The "response" (R) is 100 percent yours to choose. The "outcome" (O) becomes yours to determine.

Exercise #2
Have To, Choose To

We all have things that we have to do. Or, rather, and more accurately, we all have things that we choose to do. As you learn to release the anxiety and worry from your life, it's critical to recognize the difference.

Think about the things in life that you have to do, many of which turn into sources of anxiety. Many people would say that, among other things, you have to:

- Pay your taxes
- Take care of your children
- Get an education
- Phone your mother
- Floss your teeth

There are plenty of people, however, who don't pay their taxes, don't take care of their children, and don't phone their mothers. But, you might say, there are institutions that will make you pay your taxes, go to school, and take care of your children. And your mother might be pretty good at 'making' you phone her. You might say, further, that while it's true that there are people who don't do these things, bad things happen as a result. You're right again. But the fact remains that everyone, at all times, has a choice. And you need to be aware that, even when it feels like you are being forced into something, you still have a choice.

If we believe that there is anything at all that we absolutely, positively must do because circumstances or someone else is forcing us to, we again surrender our power. In every single instance, we hold and make the choice. Let's look at an example:

- I have to pay my taxes.
- If I don't pay my taxes, the IRS will come after me.
- If the IRS comes after me, they will freeze my accounts.
- If they freeze my accounts, I'll be broke.
- Given the choice, I'd rather pay my taxes than be broke.

But let's say you don't mind being broke ...

- It's against the law to not pay my taxes.
- If I continue to not pay, I'll be a criminal.
- If I'm a criminal, I'll go to jail.
- Given the choice, I'd rather pay my taxes than go to jail.

Of course, there are also people who would rather go to jail than pay their taxes, reveal their secret information source, renounce their beliefs, etc.

As we discovered previously, although the choices you have might not be great ones, it's absolutely critical to understand that you always have choices.

Throughout Part 1 we repeatedly made the point that worry and anxiety are choices that we make. Let's take a common example:

You're driving to work and there's a big traffic jam. You begin to worry that you're going to be late. That worry turns into a worry that, being late, you'll miss the important meeting. Which turns into a worry about the boss's opinion of you. Which turns into a worry about job security. Which turns into . . .

When you arrive late to work, you tell the boss, "The traffic made me late." In blaming the traffic, you have chosen to be a victim of circumstances beyond your control. And as you sat in the traffic jam and your blood pressure went up, you chose to blame the traffic for your blood pressure too. Both these choices leave you powerless.

Let's change things up and see if we are as much of a victim as we sometimes like to claim.

Let's say the morning's meeting was to announce you as the next Senior Vice President and the position came with a $50,000 bonus. It was conditional, however, on you being on time for the meeting. Do you think you could have found a way to be there on time? If the bonus was $500,000, would you have left the house at 3:00 a.m. or even slept in the boardroom overnight to be sure you were there? I bet you could be pretty ingenious at overcoming obstacles if we put the stakes high enough.

Which highlights the truth that you are not a victim of the traffic; you made a choice to risk the (highly predictable) heavy traffic. It was more important for you to get up at your regular time and have your regular breakfast than it was to be at the meeting on time, so you chose sleep time and breakfast over the consequences at work. Having made that choice, it's pointless to then worry about what the boss might think. If, on the other hand, you chose to make sure you were at the meeting on time, it's pointless to worry about your lost sleep.

The truth is that no one and nothing can force you to do anything. You always have the choice to comply or not, to agree or not, to act or not, to worry or not to worry. Many of us pretend we are a victim, but we are not, we always have a choice. Victim mentality, blaming, and complaining weaken our ability to make clear, conscious choices.

Have To, Choose To Worksheet

Take something you think you "have to do" and follow it through to its logical conclusion on the worksheet:

I have to (A) _____

_____

If I don't (A) _____, then (B) _____

If (B) _____, then (C) _____

If (C) _____, then (D) _____

If (D) _____, then (E) _____

If (X) _____, then (Z) _____

UNSUBSCRIBE FROM ANXIETY

I'd rather (A) _____,
than (Z)
_____

I choose to (A)
_____
_____

Since I'm choosing to (A) _____,
there is no point in me worrying about
_____

To make sure you've got the hang of it, try it again on a different situation.
I have to
_____
_____

If I don't _____, then
_____

If _____, then
_____

If _____, then
_____

If _____, then
_____

If _____, then
_____

I'd rather _____ , than
_____

I choose to
_____
_____

Since I'm choosing to _____,
there is no point in me worrying about
_____

**Remember, nobody can make you do anything!
Everything is a choice.**

9

RAISING YOUR AWARENESS

Now that you've realized the importance of and begun the practice of taking 100 percent responsibility for everything that happens in your life, the next step is to become aware of when, where, and how you worry.

There are many people who have suffered from anxiety for so long that it's become part of their 'normal.' We all breathe in and out all day long. In fact, the average person takes as many as 25,000 breaths in each twenty-four-hour period. While you can pay attention to your breathing, the vast majority of breaths are completed without any conscious assistance or awareness at all. It's so common and so normal that the act has faded completely out of our mindfulness.

Worry and anxiety, when they've gone on for

long enough to become habits, are the same. But in order for us to gain control over and, ultimately, stop the worry habit altogether, we have to become consciously aware of our worry activities. We need to observe ourselves in the act of worrying before we can gain control over it.

Who Is the 'You' That's Observing?

If you cut your finger, you can see the cut and feel the highly localized pain. Depending on its severity, that pain might be quite distracting, but you're always aware that it's your finger that hurts like heck. Your left foot feels just fine. In contrast, one of the characteristics of anxiety is that it seems to consume our entire being.

With worry and anxiety, the suffering is not localized. It affects your whole self and saps energy from your finger, your left foot, and your entire body without discrimination. As we noted earlier, they impact your ability to think clearly and gets in the way of good decision making. Our descriptions have shifted from "I have a cut," with a clear understanding that your finger is simply a small part of you, to "I am worried," as if worry is somehow who you are. Any yet, even in the midst of the deepest depression, we still somehow always retain the ability to witness ourselves experiencing the distress.

In everyday life we regularly use phrases such as "I was talking to myself," "Don't kid yourself," "I like to tell myself that . . ." Phrases like these indicate that, in addition to the "me" that goes through my daily life laughing, eating, stubbing my toe, and worrying, there is somehow another "me" that is one step removed from these activities. There's a "me" that is capable of observing all this activity without being directly involved. There is a "me" that is, in some detached way, aware of the workaday "me."

For our purposes in this book, it's not necessary to get into discussions about who this other "me" is. It's not important whether this remote "me" is somehow my soul, my higher self, or any other kind of disembodied or superconscious entity. It's enough that we're aware that this somewhat detached, third-party observer is there because that "me" is about to become really handy in helping the "day-to-day me" stop worrying.

Start Paying Closer Attention

The process begins by deciding that you're going to monitor your thoughts, especially your anxious and worried thoughts. This doesn't mean that you're going to record, verbatim, the self-talk that's going on all day between your ears. It simply means that you're going to become aware of when you find yourself worrying and what it is that you're worrying about.

This isn't about taking notes, making charts and graphs, or anything detailed like that. You're simply going to start paying attention in a way that you haven't before. Up till now you've simply worried. Your entire thinking apparatus has been wrapped up in its mentation about money, aging, relationships, health, or whatever your favorite fuss might be. From now on, though, you're going to reserve a small, separate, and detached piece of your mind whose job will be to note, "Oh, there I go worrying again. That's the third time this morning." Your job will be to observe and learn about your worry habits. It will be to simply become familiar with your anxiety patterns in a very detached, unemotional way.

At first this will be tricky. Because you're so used to your worrying habit, you do it without being aware. As you set your intention to be the observer, though, you'll find, slowly at first, that you're beginning to notice. Suddenly, in the middle of the afternoon, buried deep in the ruts of a good old-fashioned worry-fest, you'll catch yourself. "Hmmm . . . I can see that I'm worrying again."

When you do catch yourself, observe only. Don't do anything except make a mental note that you were worrying about such-and-such a topic. Don't try to change your thinking. Don't try to stop yourself from worrying. Don't try to have "detached you" interfere with "worrying you." Don't tell yourself that you shouldn't be worrying. In fact, don't judge yourself, your thoughts, or your mental state in any way at all. You're simply there as a neutral, third-party observer. All the positive changes will come soon enough.

Spending all day monitoring your thoughts can be tricky. After all, we said earlier that we can have as many as 70,000 thoughts every day and it would be impossible to keep track of them all. Fortunately, there is an easier way.

Rather than trying to pay attention to each individual thought, begin to pay attention to your feelings and your emotions. Since your emotions are the result of your thoughts, they can serve as a great indicator of where your thoughts are headed. For example, when you are occupied with worry about anything, you feel bad. It doesn't matter if the 'bad' feeling is depression, anger, jealousy, fear, or any other negative emotion. The simple fact that it feels rotten is enough to give you a heads-up that something is going on with your thoughts and you need to pay attention.

This, too, could take a little practice since you've been experiencing a steady diet of negative emotions tied to your worrying for quite a while. To be effective it's a good idea to set a two-week schedule for thought monitoring. When you wake up in the morning, remind yourself that you're going to pay attention to your worrying today. That will set a little trigger in your mind and your RAS will help out by bringing any worry thoughts to your attention. Put a note into your daily to-do list or set a reminder on your smartphone. It will only take a few days—a week at most—for you to acquire the habit of noticing when you fall into another round of worrying.

It's vital, in this phase, that you attach no judgment whatsoever to your worrying thoughts. Habits really enjoy sticking around, and if you start trying to censor your thinking too soon, you'll just encounter pushback that makes it even harder to overcome. So don't worry about your worrying. It's one step at a time, and you can reassure yourself that you've already taken many steps towards ending this annoying routine.

And Then Analyze a Little Deeper

We all have dreams and goals that we'd like to achieve. Yet far too often our worries, which are based on fears, keep us from taking action toward those goals. Perhaps there's a difficult conversation that you need to have. Perhaps there is a course you must take and a test you must pass. Maybe you need to make a presentation to a group. Whatever it is, when worry and fear set in we find ourselves imagining the worst possible outcomes.

Earlier we used an acronym to define FEAR as Fantasized Experiences Appearing Real. This is handy for remembering what we're doing to ourselves when we worry. As part of our efforts to increase our awareness of when and how we're experiencing worry, we want to become very alert to those times when we are imagining a future event and fantasizing about a horrible outcome.

You know what this feels like. You've yet to initiate the conversation, start the course, or even begin getting ready for the presentation, but you're already picturing the catastrophic outcome. The powerful images of colossal failure are swirling around your mind, your muscles are tense, your stomach is in knots, and you've begun to sweat. The fear is actually manifesting in your body because our bodies are unable to tell the difference between a real event and one that is vividly imagined. Remember, previously, how we imagined cutting into the lemon?

As you become more and more aware of those times when you're worrying, we can raise that awareness level higher. Behind all worry and anxiety is the fear that some unwanted event or consequence is going to come true. Once you've recognized that you are worrying about something, dig a little deeper and uncover the specific fear that is lying behind it. "Observer You" is going to ask "Day-to-Day You" how you're scaring yourself. What negative outcomes are you imagining? Then the two of you will work with what comes up. In this process it's vital that you be honest with yourself.

Here's how that self-talk conversation might go:

External Event: Your boss asks you to give a presentation at your next division meeting.
Day-to-Day You:
   I'm worried about this upcoming presentation.
Observer You:
   How are you scaring yourself? In other words, what are you imagining will happen?
Day-to-Day You:
   I'm imagining that I will mess it up and make a fool of myself in front of my peers. (Notice how day-to-day you is going into the future and scaring yourself with a fantasy of others laughing at you.)
Observer You:
   Have you ever made a presentation to this group before?

Day-to-Day You:
> Yes, but only once, and it was very small and inconsequential.

Observer You:
> Regardless, did you mess it up and did anyone laugh at you?

Day-to-Day You:
> No. In fact, several of them commented that I did a really good job and that they were impressed with how confident I seemed. (Notice how important it is to recall your previous victories as we did in Exercise #1.)

Observer You:
> Are you knowledgeable about the topic? Is this an opportunity to demonstrate your abilities to your boss? Is this likely to look good on your resume?

Day-to-Day You:
> Yes, yes, and yes!

Observer You:
> Have you ever done anything before that was embarrassing? And when you did (because everyone has) did you survive without permanent scarring and perhaps even grow a little?

Day-to-Day You:
> Yes, yes, and yes.

Observer You:
> So, when you think about it, this is a great opportunity to stretch your comfort zone and add to your skills and experience with no discernable downside?

Day-to-day You:
> I think I'll start working on that presentation!

Here's another scenario with a slightly different (but equally logical) outcome.

Observer You:
> I feel a knot in your stomach and I'm observing that you're worried about something.

Day-to-Day You:
> Yes. I'm worried about the big midterm exam that's coming up.

Observer You:
> How are you scaring yourself?

Day-to-Day You:
> I'm imagining that I have not studied enough and that I'll fail the exam.

Observer You:
> How much studying have you done?

Day-to-Day You:
> To be honest, not as much as I should have.

Observer You:
Then you probably have something to be concerned about. Let's make a study schedule for the next few days so you can be more prepared."
Day-to-Day You:
That feels better already!

By now you're beginning to understand how it is that we bring the unfounded fears into our lives and then reinforce them with our round-and-round mentating. By introducing Observer You into the conversation, you have found and learned to take the exit ramp from this otherwise permanent roundabout. Let's expand this a little further by working with a few more issues that bring on your anxiety.

In the next chapter you're going to make a list of things that you worry about. This won't be a list of things that you're afraid of, like flying or heights, but things that you worry about doing, such as leaving your children with a babysitter, retiring, or moving to a new job. There's a subtle, but important, difference.

For example, I worry about:

1. Applying for a promotion at work
2. Letting my teenager go out at night
3. Getting sick
4. Starting my own business

5. Asking my girlfriend to marry me
6. Hurricane season

To uncover the fear, we can take each worry and identify both the desire and the fear that are behind it by completing each sentence like this: "I want to _____, and I scare myself by imagining _____. The key words are "I scare myself by imagining."

1. I want to move up in the company, and I scare myself by imagining that I'll be passed over for a promotion.
2. I want to let my children have happy, healthy relationships, and I scare myself by imagining that they'll get into serious trouble if I don't keep them closely supervised.
3. I want to enjoy a healthy, active lifestyle, and I scare myself by imagining that I'll come down with some terrible disease.
4. I want to be my own boss, and I scare myself by imagining that I'll go out of business and have to declare bankruptcy.
5. I want to spend the rest of my life with her, and I scare myself by imagining that she'll turn me down if I ask her to marry me.
6. I want to enjoy our home on the coast, and I scare myself by imagining that a hurricane will destroy our home and kill us.

This process of learning to become aware of when we're worrying and then identifying the fear that lies behind the worry teaches us to pull the worrying habit back out of our subconscious, daily 'normal' and into the realm of 'front-of-mind.' If you've tried a few of these mental exercises, you might already be feeling more detached from and ready to be in control of the anxious thoughts that seem to invade and occupy your mind, leaving you feeling so awful.

Exercise #3
Can't or Won't?

Let's play with this idea of personal choice a little more.

A twelve-month-old baby knows a lot about failure. Every time she lets go of the coffee table to attempt a step or two—thump! Failed again. Of course the easiest way for our cute little one to avoid failure is to give up on the idea of walking. It would be so much easier to just sit and let Mom bring the bottle.

There are a couple of reasons why that toddler keeps trying. First, the world looks pretty big and exciting, and you can cover a lot more ground on two feet than on all fours, so it's worth the effort. But more importantly, she hasn't yet got the memo that failure is a bad thing. There's no shame in falling on your butt when you're twelve months old. In fact we grown-ups think it's pretty darn cute.

Our brain is designed to do everything it can to ensure our survival. But as we get older it behaves more and more like an overprotective parent and prevents us from trying things that will actually result in our growth. We've all tried things that were new, daring, and adventurous, most often in our childhood and youth. Occasionally those daring adventures ended badly—with a skinned knee, an embarrassment, or a financial loss. In other cases a parent or teacher caught us as we were about to embark on the adventure and, with great hysteria, related all the horrid things that would befall us if we were so stupid as to go ahead with that hairbrained scheme.

By the time we've grown up, been formally educated, gotten a job, and taken responsibility for ourselves, our family, our children ... the world has managed to thoroughly convince us that failure is the worst possible option, to be avoided at all costs. And that's when most growth and learning stops. We learned to be less adventurous, less daring and gradually convinced ourselves that there are many things that we simply can't do, and therefore, won't try.

Most people spend an inordinate effort to avoid failure of any kind. Which, don't get me wrong, is a pretty good idea when you're flying a plane or doing heart surgery. But it's a major obstacle when you're trying to grow as a person. By assiduously avoiding failure, we also avoid innovation, creativity, growth, and breakthrough thinking. We stay carefully in the rut we occupy and discourage looking from side to side.

Those people, on the other hand, that we all respect and wish we could be like—well, they encourage, embrace, and endure failure on their way to the successes the rest of us admire. And the faster they fail, the quicker they grow.

We've talked at length about how our fears, anxieties, and worries have turned into beliefs that we hold about ourselves. Some of them are emboldening and uplifting. But, unfortunately, too many have become roadblocks to our success.

Far too much of our 'self-talk' reinforces our self-limiting, success-blocking beliefs.

- "You shouldn't do that, it'll cost way too much money!"
- "There's no chance she'll go out with you. She's way out of your league."
- "Start your own business? Don't be an idiot!"

These are all examples of 'victim language,' the kind of statements uttered by those who are beaten, defeated, and crushed. Is it true that we are actually incapable of achieving these dreams? Or have we simply bought into the propaganda that the world has been feeding us since we were first told, "You'll put your eye out!" Let's start to remove those roadblocks by developing new habits in the way we talk to ourselves.

Begin by making a list of things that you can't do. For example, your list might include:

- I can't run a marathon.

- I can't climb Mount Everest.
- I can't make a million dollars.
- I can't leave this toxic relationship.
- I can't stop worrying.

Go ahead and make your list here. Use your journal if you prefer. When you're finished, read your statements out loud to yourself and really put the feeling of "I can't!" into them.

1. I can't _____

2. I can't _____

3. I can't _____

4. I can't _____

5. I can't _____

When you're finished, take a moment and think about the feelings that are aroused as you spoke those statements. Did you feel strong? Empowered? Successful? Or did you feel defeated and somewhat helpless? For most people, statements of "I can't . . ." bring on strong feelings of powerlessness, fatigue, and weakness.

Now let's begin a gradual transition. Take your same statements, only this time, instead of beginning the sentence with "I can't," replace it with "I won't!" For example:

- I won't run a marathon!
- I won't climb Mount Everest!
- I won't make a million dollars!
- I won't leave this toxic relationship!
- I won't stop worrying!

Again, read your statements out loud and be sure to put the strong feeling of "I won't!" into them.

How do your feelings while making these statements differ from before? Did you have a sense of being slightly more in control? Did you begin to have the feeling that the decision and the choice belongs to you instead of someone or something else? This is the beginning of an important shift in power. Instead of events, circumstances, and people outside of you dictating what will and won't happen, *you* are the one making those decisions. And this is the beginning of the end of your worry and anxiety.

Let's carry on with some even more powerful and dynamic self-talk.

Take your same statements, only this time, let's replace "I won't" with "I'll try to . . ." For example:

- I'll try to run a marathon!
- I'll try to climb Mount Everest!
- I'll try to make a million dollars!
- I'll try to leave this toxic relationship!
- I'll try to stop worrying!

Say them out loud and feel the beginning stirrings of possibility. Suddenly your mind is open to the prospect that it just might be conceivable. Can you feel an uplifting in your spirit? Let's take yet another step.

Now begin your statements with "I will . . ." and see how the feelings change.

- I will run a marathon!
- I will climb Mount Everest!
- I will make a million dollars!
- I will leave this toxic relationship!
- I will stop worrying!

Now you're setting an intent. As soon as you do that, and you infuse that intent with the emotions of determination, pride, and confidence, your reticular activating system (remember your RAS?) and your energy vibrations go to work, looking for and seeking out events, opportunities, resources, and reinforcements that come to your aid in achieving these goals you've set for yourself.

And let's take one final step in the change to your self-talk. This time, instead of allowing even the slightest hesitation into your statements, remove every last vestige of uncertainty by beginning each statement with "I can!"

Because of course you can! You may not want to, you may not choose to. But, should you decide to, you absolutely can . . .

- run a marathon!
- climb Mount Everest!
- make a million dollars!
- leave this toxic relationship!
- stop worrying!

The choice and the power reside entirely with you. You don't need anyone's permission or approval. You don't need to justify or convince. You simply need to decide.

None of this means that running a marathon or leaving a toxic relationship will be without effort—although you may very well find, if you choose to pursue any of those goals, that it's far easier than you ever would have imagined. Once you discover that the biggest obstacle to your success has been your own self-limiting beliefs, you become free to try and succeed or even to try and fail at whatever suits your fancy.

Have you ever pulled out of a parking spot, driven along the street for a distance, and couldn't figure out why the car wouldn't go like it should? Then you looked down and realized that you'd left the parking brake on. Release it and the car is free to cruise down the interstate at speeds that will get you arrested if you want.

There is no need to hold on to the self-doubts you've been carrying for far too long. There is no need to suffer the debilitating effects of negative experiences from long ago that continue to hold you back. That old comfort zone is too small to hold you now. Those old beliefs about what you can or should do, those old guilts and self-doubts don't fit you anymore.

The choices are yours. The choices have always been yours.

10

TAKING INVENTORY

Sooner or later, every one of us gets fed up with worrying, hiding under the bed, and surrendering command of our lives. In spite of the power those demons wield, it's entirely possible to remove those roadblocks. Since it's all self-imposed, we can learn to unplug from the fear. We can untangle the net of fear, anxiety, and self-doubt that keeps us from exploring our limitless human potential. We can live up to the promises we've made to ourselves.

Anyone can do it. But only if you're willing to hit that 'off' switch. Only if you want to leave the drama behind and get to know the valuable, competent, courageous, remarkable human being that you are.

Get It Down on Paper

The first step in leaving your worries behind is

to establish an accurate assessment of exactly what it is you're anxious about and how this worry routine began. When reflecting on my own life and the worry habits that I wanted to leave behind, I discovered a number of origins and reinforcements that needed to be addressed.

For example, I've mentioned that I did not grow up with anything even approaching financial wealth. We were wealthy in many non-financial ways, but dollars were scarce. One of the ways that my parents dealt with the situation was that my mother would sew many of our clothes herself. While it was a tremendous amount of work, not to mention a tremendous talent, as a young child I was always conscious of and embarrassed about wearing homemade clothes instead of fancy store-bought ones like the other kids wore. This was one of the many situations that reinforced for me that money didn't grow on trees and needed to be worried about constantly.

As I turned all these sources of fear and worry over and over in my mind, that's all that seemed to happen—I turned them over and over in my mind. I never made progress with my thinking. I never came up with any solutions. I simply regurgitated the same mental contents of yesterday, last week, last month, last year again and again.

Painful, boring, and not the least bit useful.

One day, I was somehow inspired to take the constantly recurring thoughts out of my brain and put them down on paper. And that's when everything began to change. All of a sudden, as I reread the notes I'd made, the worries weren't inside my head, they had somehow moved outside of me. I had gained an objectivity about them that hadn't existed when they were simply swirling around in my brain. Suddenly, my worried thoughts no longer owned me. I owned them. And now that I owned them, they were mine to do with, to control and to dispose of, as I pleased.

A major success strategy in conquering your own anxieties and worries is to get them outside of you, to externalize those feelings. And one of the most effective ways of doing this is to write your feelings, and the origins of those feelings, down on paper.

So now it's your turn. As I mentioned at the beginning of the book, I encourage you to start a personal journal in which to do the exercises and keep track of your progress. As you work through the process of transcending your anxieties, keep your notebook handy because as you set your mind to the task of letting your worries go, important ideas, understandings, and revelations will occur to you that represent forward movement. It will help your progress if you write them down. Call it your

"Worry-Free Journal" if you want.

While it might be tempting to use your computer or tablet, it's far more effective to write your list out on paper by hand than it is to type it into a computer. While the computer might be faster and more convenient, there's something about the slower, more deliberate and kinesthetic act of writing that helps you objectify and externalize these negative emotions, which is an important part of the letting-go process. As you write, imagine the anxieties flowing out through your arm, your hand, and your fingers, into the pen and onto the paper.

As you write, you can fully expect your self-censor to spring into action and try to shut you down or at least minimize your efforts. You'll find your self-talk saying things such as "This really isn't a problem for me." "It's really not that bad." "I should be able to stop worrying on my own." "Maybe it's not just simply anxiety. Maybe I need medication." "What would my (mother) (husband) (rabbi) (children) say if they knew I was struggling with this?" "This is just silly! I've got more important things to do." "My anxieties aren't worth this much attention. Think about the starving children..."

Recognize these thoughts as they arise and smile as you recall that we predicted them right here. Don't fight them, but let them gently pass through and then out of your mind. Imagine these thoughts as wisps of mist that drift into your brain and then drift right back out again. No need to pay them any attention.

The fact is that you do deserve to live a worry-free life. You are worthy of the time and attention it takes to let your anxieties melt away. You have as much right to a joyful, fear-free life as anyone, and it's time to be kind and gentle with yourself. So let all the "shoulds," "ought tos," and "you're doing whats?!" that come your way roll right off your back. This is your Me Time and you deserve it.

Use your journal to list your most persistent worry topics. Make your statements simple, but factual. Don't try to justify, explain, or judge yourself in any way. Just write them out. As you write about each worry topic and its origins, allow yourself to again feel fully the emotions that you felt way back then as you were told or witnessed something that caused you to begin to be anxious. Feel, also, the emotions you experience every time a present-day trigger reinforces that anxiety. Let your thoughts flow into words on the paper as you freely describe your feelings.

Here are some examples to help you get underway.

I worry that:

- I won't have enough money for retirement
- My husband is going to stop finding me attractive
- I won't get into a good college
- The Baby Boomers are going to bankrupt Social Security
- If I don't lose this weight I'll have a heart attack
- Global warming is going to result in mass famine
- I will look foolish in front of my business colleagues
- I'll be rejected when I ask for something
- People will criticize me for my opinions

Let your list be as long or as short as it needs to be. If you find yourself, on some kind of regular basis, worrying, fretting, anxious, or otherwise bothered about anything, put it on the list. We'll deal with them all in turn.

It's also okay to come back and add something to the list that you think of later or to repeat the exercise at a later date. If you are in the habit of worrying about any one particular topic, it's highly likely that you find yourself anxious about other things too. It's not the external event or circumstance that causes the worry, it's our emotional response to it. A robust worry habit loves to find more and more things to fret about and as you write your list you'll find yourself loosening up, being more forthright with yourself, and recognizing the full breadth of this anxiety habit. This exercise is to get it all out on the paper.

Put the book down, pick up your pen and your journal, and start making your list now.

Next, I'm going to ask you a series of questions and I want you to write out your answers in your journal. You might want to have a separate page or two for each worry topic so that you have plenty of room to expand on the thoughts that occur to you. Take your time with this and be sure to note anything that comes into your mind. The more detail you can provide, the better.

1. *Why is this a worry for you?*

The best way to answer this question is to use the phrase we adopted in the previous chapter: "How are you scaring yourself?" So for each item on your worry list, work through the following process.

I'm worried about _____. I'd really like to _____, and I scare myself by imagining _____ if I did.

2. *How did this first start to be a worry for you?*

Was there a particular event that set it off? Were there circumstances with your family, childhood friends, or religious upbringing that convinced you there are things about which you should rightly be worried? What did you learn from your parents, relatives, friends, teachers, religious leaders, coaches that has led you to believe that these worries are necessary?

The teaching may have been very direct. For example, a parent who suffered a traumatic experience of their own might have passed on their belief that all strangers are to be mistrusted. Or the teaching may have been subtler, as the bully in the playground used slurs and innuendoes that reinforced sexual stereotypes.

Try to recall specific events or circumstances that you observed as you were growing up that had a worrying impact on you and caused you to feel less secure or less worthy. For each instance, use your journal to describe the training, the incident, event, or circumstances that got you started thinking that you ought to be worried.

Here are some examples that might trigger your own recollections.

- Parents who were always concerned that there wasn't enough money
- Being chosen last for pick-up sports games
- A father who told about the time he was mugged and now any news report about a mugging recalls and reinforces the fears

3. *How long have you been worrying about this?*

Can you recall when you began to have this issue as a regular cause for anxiety? Is it relatively recent, say within the last few weeks or months? Or has it been a worry of yours for a six months, a year, or more?

4. *How often do you find yourself with this worry occupying your mind?*

Would you say that it's daily? Every two or three days? More than once a day? Hourly? Or is this worry a virtual nonstop presence in your mind?

5. *Is there anything in particular that triggers your anxiety?*

If you have an allergy—perhaps to gluten, or dust and pollen—they reliably trigger your runny nose, itchy eyes, or stomachache. Are there any particular things, events, circumstances, or even people that set you to worrying when you might have otherwise been enjoying a great day?

6. *How intense is your discomfort when you're worrying or anxious?*

Worry and anxiety feel awful. Since one of your goals is to feel better, it would be handy to have some way to measure just how awful you feel when you're anxious in order to judge your progress in letting it all go. Developed in 1969 by psychiatrist

Joseph Wolpe, the Subjective Units of Distress Scale (or SUDS) is a 0-to-10 scale for measuring the intensity of the disturbance you feel. Since your distress is something that you, and only you can feel, the SUDS is a great tool for you to self-assess. There are no strict rules by which you self-assign a SUDS rating to your anxiety. That's why it's called "subjective."

To use the scale, simply ask yourself, "On a scale of zero to ten, where zero is the best I can feel and ten is the worst, how do I feel right now?" The point of the question is to let you notice your own improvement, so there's no benefit in trying to compare your score with that of your friend. As you continue to document this analysis in your journal, give yourself a SUDS score for each of the worries you've identified.

Here is one version of the scale*:

0 *Completely peaceful and serene. You don't feel anxiety of any kind.*
1 *You feel pretty good. If you really thought about it you might find something that's sort of bothering you, but not much.*
2 *You're a little bit upset, but it's not really noticeable until you think about it.*
3 *You can tell that you're a little upset or anxious and you definitely notice it.*

4 *You are somewhat upset and you can't easily ignore the unpleasant thoughts. You've got it under control but it doesn't feel good.*

5 *You're upset to the point that it's uncomfortable. The feelings are definitely unpleasant, but with some effort you can manage them.*

6 *Your bad feelings have reached the point that you begin to think something needs to be done about it*

7 *You're very anxious and distressed. This is getting in the way of you being able to perform your daily duties.*

8 *Now you're freaking out. You're very distressed and you've lost the ability to concentrate.*

9 *You are feeling desperate and extremely freaked out to the point that it's almost unbearable.*

10 *Feels unbearably bad, beside yourself, out of control as in a nervous breakdown, overwhelmed, at the end of your rope.*

*Copyright – The concept of this scale was originally developed by Joseph Volpe in 1969. Because it is purposely subjective, various versions and interpretations of it have been developed by many others since and are commonly used in cognitive-behavioral therapy. It is particularly useful for assessing anxiety disorders. As far as we know, there is no copyright regarding this scale and you may freely copy and use this version.

Acknowledgment: Wolpe, Joseph, The Practice of Behavior Therapy, New York, Pergamon Press, 1969

7. *What will happen if this worry comes true?*

Go ahead, fantasize about the worst possible outcomes you imagine. Let all your fears flow out here and tell your journal about the rat-infested prison, the homelessness, or the deadly disease. Please don't play self-censor on this as it's really important that you're honest with yourself about the fears that simmer within you, frequently below your level of awareness.

8. *What is the likelihood of this actually coming to pass?*

When you ask the third-party, objective observer "you" this question, you're likely to get a more realistic answer. And it's highly likely that the chances of your worst fears coming true are pretty slim. As we noted previously, when we talked about Fantasized Experiences Appearing Real, most of our fears and worries exist exclusively in our imagination.

9. *Has it ever come to pass before?*

Many of the things we worry about actually never have and never will happen. Has this particular worry ever turned into a reality for you?

10. *If yes, what lessons did you learn from the experience?*

The fact that you're alive, reading this book, proves that you survived the experience, and every challenge brings important lessons. What did you learn from going through the experience that helped you grow? What did you learn that may have increased or caused additional worries? Are there things that you could be doing differently now to prevent, or reduce, the likelihood of it happening again?

Great! How did it feel to write about your worries? As you described them, analyzed them and documented them, did it generate any sense of detachment from the feelings that those worries generate in you? Now that you've completed this journaling exercise, does it feel as if the SUDS score you first assigned each worry might have gone down a point or two?

Quite often, the very act of objectively identifying and rendering your worry topics into writing, allowing you to look at and assess them in the cold light of day, begins to distance you from them and their power over you. If you didn't sense those beginning feelings of objectivity, don't worry. There's more to come.

11

LETTING ANXIETY GO

Now it's time to release and say goodbye to your worry and anxiety.

As you get ready to let your anxiety go, I encourage you to think in terms of releasing and letting go of it rather than defeating or overcoming it. If you think of your anxiety as an 'enemy' that must be vanquished in some kind of battle, it will be much more difficult. When we push against anything, it always pushes back and resists our efforts. But if, instead, we simply let go, surrender, and release, it drifts away without any effort on our part.

Up to this point we've been studying and analyzing the way in which fear and worry originate, how our thinking habits reinforce them, and how most of what we fear and worry about are, actually, self-generated mental fantasies. Since fear, worry, anxiety, and self-doubt are built from mental habits, they can't be removed with a surgeon's scalpel. And while they might, for a while, be camouflaged by medication, the underlying root of the problem can only be permanently removed through mental work that you, and only you, can do.

It was your mental activities that first brought worry to you and it's your ongoing mental habits that keep it hanging around. So it only makes sense that we'll need to release and ultimately let it go through a different set of mental activities. We're going to be using guided visualization to go deep inside to where the worry and anxiety reside. We're going to take charge of it, we're going to take it outside ourselves, and then we're going to release it. Permanently.

Remember earlier, when we visualized cutting into the lemon and your mouth began to salivate? That was because your body, which includes your brain, can't tell the difference between something that is real and something that is vividly imagined. Visualization is a process that takes advantage of the combined power of your conscious and subconscious minds. It uses the power of your imagination to 'see' your desired outcome in your mind's eye in a way that is so powerful, it becomes for you a new reality.

Visualization, also sometimes called guided imagery, is a way of creating a detailed mental image of an object, a place, or a situation that you find desirable. Sometimes, if you want to reduce stress, you can simply visualize an attractive and peaceful setting and your body will respond by relaxing. Or perhaps you want to inspire yourself to action. Visualizing an outcome that you're working towards keeps your mind focused on the goal and motivates you when the going gets tough. In our case, we're going to use visualization to release the worry and anxiety that seem to occupy us.

Guided imagery is useful in a number of other ways as well. First, it's frequently combined with relaxation techniques, which will be helpful in releasing the tension that is always associated with anxiety. Second, it involves an element of distraction, which can redirect your attention away from your worry and toward those things that uplift and empower you. Finally, visualization provides a nonverbal instruction or direct suggestion to your body, your unconscious mind, and your RAS to act "as if" your worry-free state already exists.

The kind of visualization we'll be using can also be thought of as a form of guided meditation. Like any meditation technique, part of the goal is to learn how to detach ourselves from the moment-to-moment frenzy of mental activity that we can't seem to stop. Instead, we learn to detach, in a relaxed way, from that steady stream of thought and simply observe our thoughts as they float in and then back out of our consciousness. This is a long way from that nonstop mentation that is uncontrolled worry and anxiety.

The final benefit of visualization that I want to mention before we dive into it is that it's highly portable. Anywhere you are, any time of the day, you can take a few moments to close your eyes and call upon your ability to imagine. Of course, it's best done in a peaceful setting that's free from distraction, but, in a pinch, a thirty-second elevator ride or the commute on a city bus can provide a delightful mental oasis in the middle of a busy day.

You can read through the following instructions, familiarize yourself with them, and then go ahead and do the visualization. A more effective way, though, might be to record the instructions in your own voice on your smartphone and then play it back as you go through the exercise. If you choose to record yourself, read the instructions in a calm, relaxed voice without hurrying.

Let's get to it.

Anxiety-Releasing Visualization

- Find a private, calm, and quiet space and sit comfortably in a chair with your eyes closed. Let your back be comfortably straight with your feet on the ground. Your hands can rest gently in your lap or on your thighs.
- Begin by selecting the specific worry topic that you'd like to release during this session. Perhaps it's money, health, a relationship, or something else. Spend a few moments reflecting on the things you learned about this particular worry in the last chapter, including its origins, its intensity, and its frequency. As you think about the worry, be sure to maintain that objective, third-party observer view, without being drawn back into an emotional response to the topic.
- When you're ready with your topic, take a few slow and deep breaths and focus on feeling the inhalation and exhalation.
- Become aware of the feeling of your back resting against the back of your chair; the sensation of your hips and thighs on the seat of your chair, your feet on the floor. Become aware, also, of the rise and fall of your chest and stomach as you let your breathing find its own natural rhythm.
- With every exhale, allow one part of your body to relax. Breathe in, and as you breathe out, let the muscles of your shoulders relax. Feel those

muscles go limp. Next, breathe in, and as you breathe out, let the muscles in your arms relax. Then, with each subsequent breath, slowly work your way through your entire body—your chest muscles, your hips, your thighs, your knees, your ankles, your feet. Finally, let the muscles in your face and your scalp relax.

- Feel your steady, relaxed breathing and allow your body to enjoy the state of relaxation for a few moments.
- Now begin to shift your attention to the topic of worry that you've chosen to release. Let yourself ponder the worry and feel it begin to occupy your mind and your body. Put yourself into a place where you can feel the emotion of it in your body.
- Focus on the physical feeling of the worry in your body. What is the dominant sensation you are feeling? Is it a tension in your muscles? Is it a feeling of heat? Is it a vibration of some sort? Identify and isolate the physical sensation of the worry in your body.
- Where is the sensation located? Is it in your neck and shoulders? Your jaw? Your abdominal area? Your buttocks? Allow yourself to feel the very specific location of this sensation in your body and focus on that for a few moments.

- As you increase your awareness of this physical sensation in your body, begin to think about how you might describe it. If it's in your neck and shoulders, does it reach fully from one shoulder tip to the other? Is it just between your shoulder blades? Is it a tight, focused knot or is it broader and more generalized? How would you describe this sensation?
- Now that it is taking shape in your mind, begin to imagine it as a physical object. Visualize that object and become familiar with it. What shape is it? Is it round? Oblong? Square? How tall is it? What part, and how much of your body does it occupy?
- It is warmer or colder than the rest of your body? Is it hard or soft? Solid or hollow?
- What would it feel like to touch it? Is it smooth or rough? Does it have a texture? What color is it?
- Now that you have a really good image of this worry-object in your body, spend a few moments just observing it. Imagine seeing it from the front, from the back and the side. Walk around it and examine it like you might look at a piece of sculpture with its shape and texture and size and color.

- Once you've become completely familiar with this worry-object, use your mind and imagination to begin manipulating it. Start by making it as large as you can. Whatever shape it is, imagine it getting bigger and bigger until it reaches the limits of your body. Let it be big for a few moments, and then begin to shrink it. Watch as it gets smaller and smaller, back to its original size, and then continue to shrink it until it's quite tiny, almost too small to see. Now bring it back to its original size.
- Now use your imagination to spin it around. Slowly at first but then faster and faster. Watch this object spin inside you, then slow it down again and bring it to a stop.
- Next, begin to move this object around inside your body. First move it slowly up to your right shoulder and then down your arm. Feel it moving down your arm, past your elbow, down to your wrist, and then into your hand. Let it rest there for a few moments.
- Bring it back up your right arm to your shoulder, then move it diagonally down across your chest and abdomen to your left hip. Then slowly move it down your left leg, past your knee, and down to your foot.
- Begin to be playful with this worry-object, moving it around inside your body, bouncing it back

and forth like you might a ball. Let it be a fun exercise of moving it around, spinning it, expanding and then shrinking it at will.
- When you've had enough fun moving it around inside your body, take it back up to the shoulder of your dominant hand—right or left—and then move it down your arm to your hand. This time, let it come out of your body and rest in the palm of your hand. Wrap your fingers around it, feeling its texture and temperature. Feel the weight of it in your hand and bounce it up and down a few times like you might with a baseball.
- Now, holding it in your hand, reach down and set it on the floor beside your chair. Use your imagination and your mind's eye to look down at it on the floor beside you. Let it sit there on the floor for a few moments.
- Now visualize picking it back up and holding it in your hand again.
- As you hold it in your hand, watch as this object slowly begins to become less and less solid. It gradually becomes more vaporous, almost as if it's dissolving. Instead of being a firm, dense object, it increasingly looks as if it's made of dust or smoke. It's getting lighter and lighter in your hand.
- When it has dissolved to the point that you can almost see through it, pause and just look at this

thin, wispy, vaporous thing in your hand. It's weightless, it has no substance, it has no power. It is virtually nothing at all.
- Now take a deep breath and blow really hard on it, like you'd blow out a whole cake full of birthday candles.
- Watch as this now ghost-like object dissolves, vaporizes, and blows away like dust in the wind as it disappears into nothingness.
- Watch the final wisps of dust disappear.
- Return your attention to your relaxed breathing. Feel the soft inhale and exhale and the gentle rise and fall of your chest.
- When you're ready, taking as much time as you need, begin to gently stretch—first your fingers and toes, then your arms and legs, becoming slowly aware, once again, of being in your body on your chair.
- Take as long as you need, then, when you're ready, take a big breath and on the exhalation slowly open your eyes and gently come back into the room.

After you have reoriented yourself for a few minutes, think about how you feel. Go back to that place in your body where you felt the anxiety. How does it feel now? Is it still there? If it is, what SUDS score would you give it now?

If you feel up to it, try to feel worried about your topic again. Is it harder now to be worried? Do you feel a greater sense of ease and peace? If you can still feel some remnants of the anxiety, is it in charge of you? Or are you in charge of it? Now who is controlling what?

You can repeat this exercise for any other worry topic you have or any time you find that anxiety is trying to come back.

12

WHAT'S THE WORST THAT COULD HAPPEN?

Congratulations! You're now able to take those fantasized fears, gently assume control, and then release them from occupying your mind and your body. While you might not have completely eliminated the worry, you've reduced it significantly. Should you want to reduce it even further, should it return or should other worries arise, you now have the skills to analyze them objectively, see them for the imaginary threats they are, and gently persuade them to leave.

Now that you've learned how to take control of your worries and let them go, it's time to learn how to deal with a different kind of anxiety—the kind that comes from events that are highly likely to or actually do turn out to be real.

The world is a wonky place, where crazy—sometimes unpleasant and even painful—things happen. Yes, even to good people. How you respond when it all hits the fan, though, is what makes all the difference for your peace of mind.

To begin this process I want to take you back to Chapter 10, where we talked about the importance of taking 100 percent responsibility for everything that happens to you. We began that chapter by saying that it is essential to master this principle first because everything that follows is based on and requiring of this practice being solidly in place.

The opposite of taking 100 percent responsibility is blaming and complaining about the situations life hands us and the circumstances in which we find ourselves. While it might be easier and, at least temporarily, more satisfying to look for someone or something to blame for our misfortune, it accomplishes exactly nothing to help you out of it. In fact, it completely removes any power you might have to improve or resolve the situation. If you decide that the fault lies with your boss, the government, or the weather, you're left hoping that one of them will change in order to improve conditions in your life. And that's not going to happen any time soon.

While it might very well be the weather, the government, or your boss that created a circumstance that isn't beneficial to you, when you decide to own the situation, you take back the power to control and change it. You have the choice in how you respond and, in that choice, lies all your power.

Let me give you a couple of examples:

Moving the Goalposts

In the early 1990s I was offered an exciting job with a company in Boston. The opportunity was truly once-in-a-lifetime, and it gave me the chance to play at a whole new level that I'd never be able to get to on my own. I was born and raised in Canada, so the job required that I emigrate to the USA.

I sold my house in Toronto, packed up everything, and relocated. Shortly after starting at the new company, the boss called me into his office and said that he was going to change the rules of the game. Instead of a reliable salary, he was going to switch me to a commission-based income.

I had a four-year-old and a seven-year-old at home. I had an immigration visa that allowed me to work for this, and only this, company. And I had a boss who was pulling the rug out from underneath me. I had three choices: 1) blame and complain about how I'd been duped, 2) go along with what amounted to extortion, or 3) quit and try to find another way to support my family. None of the choices were appealing, but I did have choices.

I admit to spending some time with choice number one, but ultimately, I left that company and launched my own. There's no doubt that it was tough going and even scary for a while. But every morning I woke up empowered by the knowledge that my success did not depend on someone else's decision. It rested entirely in my hands. When it's all up to you, you are capable of remarkable things.

Winter in O'Hare Airport
A great deal of my career has involved travel, so I'm familiar with almost every airport in the country. Some more than others. On one occasion I was working with a client in Chicago for a few days. It was time to head home just as a major winter storm hit the east coast.

It was one of those storms that seemed to paralyze the entire country, and my flight was cancelled. Not to worry, I'd get a hotel room and catch a flight the next day. The problem was that O'Hare Airport held thousands of people whose flights had also been cancelled and had managed to snag the available hotels before I did. So I slept on a bench in the airport.

The next day was spent standing in lines that were hours long, only to be told that no flights were available. No hotel rooms either. I finally got home after spending three nights sleeping on benches in the airport and standing in endless lines.

Here was a case in which the cause of my problem was the weather, and I was left with no practical choices for a solution. While I couldn't change the situation, I could change my attitude about it. Getting angry, frustrated, or rude was pointless and would only raise my blood pressure.

So I chose to be chill about it and it made all the difference. It didn't change the conditions one bit, but my choice to own my feelings and my decision to have those feelings be calm, peaceful, and even amused, allowed me to experience an otherwise awful situation in a relaxed and worry-free state.

I still spend a lot of time in airports and I frequently see people who are borderline apoplectic with anger, anxiety, and worry that they'll miss their connection or be otherwise inconvenienced. They are beside themselves with worry that they'll miss their flight.

So what?

People miss flights all the time. And when they do, the meeting gets postponed, the party is missed, or the vacation begins one day later. Again, so what?

People actually lose their jobs all the time too. They also get sick all the time, and they suffer the breakup of relationships too. If you're alive and breathing, bad things are, occasionally, going to happen to you. But you are going to survive.

The point is, we spend so much time worrying about horrible things happening to us. And on the odd occasion when they do, it's never so bad as we believe it's going to be. Yes, it's inconvenient, even annoying. But the feelings of tension, anxiety, anger, and frustration that we experience by letting ourselves be rattled by the anticipation of the event are far more disturbing, damaging, and dangerous than the unwelcome outcomes that we endure.

Remember the list of negative health effects that worry and anxiety can bring on? Here's a quick reminder: Skin conditions, irritability, high blood pressure, ulcers, restlessness, panic attacks, increased heart rate, hyperventilation, sweating, trembling, feeling weak or tired, trouble concentrating, gastrointestinal problems, depression, headaches, irritability, heart palpitations, muscle aches, and loss of libido.

Or you could just be late for your meeting. The choice is yours.

The same comparison is true regardless of the particular worry that might be your personal favorite. We all believe that our worry is different, the negative outcomes more catastrophic, the consequences more far-reaching. But they're not.

While the negative outcomes are never as bad as we believe they're going to be, the lessons that we can learn and the growth we can experience from those outcomes are always infinitely more valuable than you can imagine. But that's if, and only if, we choose to pay attention to the lessons.

Let's look at my two horrible-outcome stories and weigh the negative versus positive outcomes.

Getting duped by my boss

Negative Outcomes	*Positive Outcomes*
Lost my job	Learned to read contracts more carefully
Suffered a few sleepless nights	Increased my mental flexibility
	Increased my problem-solving skills
	Learned to stay cool in challenging situations
	Became more self-reliant
	Acquired new business skills
	Improved my sales skills
	Became more mature
	Significantly expanded my comfort zone
	Started my own business

Three nights in O'Hare Airport

Negative Outcomes	*Positive Outcomes*
Kinks in my neck	Learned that your

A few extra nights away from home	worst nightmare is never as bad as you imagine
	Learned that gate agents hold all the power
	Learned that being nice to gate agents gets you better treatment than being nasty
	Learned that anxiety feels far worse than a few kinks in your neck
	Learned to build flexibility and patience into business travel—especially in winter
	Hours of entertaining people-watching
	Free time to get some extra work done
	Three new novels read

Think back to some situations in which the very thing you were worried about came true. While it's obvious that you survived, how bad was it? Be honest with your assessment here—did things turn out to be as terrible as you had imagined them being during the runup to the catastrophe? Or were they not quite as awful as you anticipated they were going to be?

Perhaps, more importantly, did you grow from the experience? Did you learn any lessons that have helped you to avoid or mitigate similar situations in the future? What were your takeaways? Did it just leave you even more worried about a repeat performance? Or did experiencing the consequence result in your being better prepared and better equipped in the future?

There is no doubt that at some point in your future, something is going to happen that you'd prefer didn't. Are you going to spend the time between now and that day working on your heart palpitations? Or are you going to rationally anticipate that life will throw the occasional curveball, be ready with the lessons you've been learning all your life and, in the meantime, enjoy the sunshine?

> *Do you remember the things you were worrying about a year ago? How did they work out? Didn't you waste a lot of fruitless energy on account of most of them? Didn't most of them turn out all right after all?*
> *—Dale Carnegie*

Part 3—Living a Worry-Free Life

Here's the thing—in the same way that you can't live your entire life without experiencing the occasional bad weather day, it's impossible to completely avoid all fear. Fear is a natural—and useful—response to unknown or threatening situations.

Worry and anxiety, though, are completely optional and your life would be much happier, more peaceful, and more successful without them. In this section you're going to see what a worry-free life can look like. You're also going to learn the three vital keys to achieving and maintaining your worry-free status. Finally, you're going to discover the new mental habits that will replace your old habits of worry, anxiety, and self-doubt.

It's a wonderful, worry-free world and you're invited into it.

13

WHAT DOES WORRY-FREE" FEEL LIKE?

Wow! Do we ever need to stop worrying and just chill!

Check out this data collected in the National Health and Nutrition Examination Survey by the Centers for Disease Control and Prevention (CDC).

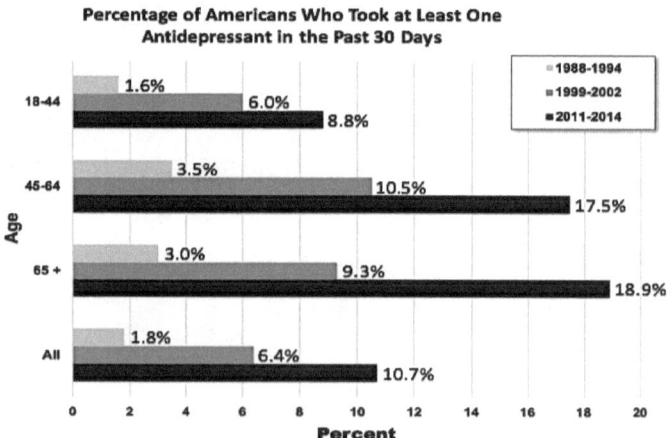

Source: NCHS, National Health and Nutrition Examination Survey

Previously we talked about how catch-phrases such as "anxiety epidemic," "Prozac nation," and "anxiety consumerism" have been coined by the media. But behind the headlines, the statistics on our national decline into depression are just out of hand:

- The number of Americans who say they've taken an antidepressant over the past month rose by 65 percent between 1999 and 2014.
- Nearly 7 percent of all prescriptions filled are for anxiety or depression medications.
- Overdose deaths involving drugs commonly used to treat anxiety quadrupled between 2002 and 2015.
- The market for benzos, short for benzodiazepines, one of the primary anxiety and depression medications, is expected to reach $3.8 billion in the US by 2020.

In the face of these overwhelming trends, is it actually possible to live worry-free? In spite of our current obsession with worry and anxiety, and the constant bombardment of worry-inducing information, the answer is, emphatically, *yes!* And, not only is it possible, it's healthier, more productive, more creative, more successful, and much, much more joyful.

Let's be clear: A worry-free life is not and should

not be a fear-free life.

Fear is a natural and extremely useful response that humans share with many, much simpler organisms. I live in a neighborhood that is heavily wooded, and we share the area with a very healthy population of white-tailed deer. These animals are notoriously nervous and run at the slightest sign of danger. But, like all species with some level of intelligence, they're also able to learn. It's been interesting to watch as the deer have slowly come to realize that humans (at least in this neighborhood) are not a threat and the deer comfortably stand and watch as we walk or drive by.

You're much smarter than any white-tailed deer and capable of learning much more complex concepts, much more quickly. Throughout your life, one of the patterns of your learning has been to decrease the number of things that you're afraid of. When you were a very young child, you might have been scared of the dark, thunder, and even Santa Claus. When you were older, you were afraid to jump off the high board at the swimming pool, ask a girl (or a boy) to dance, and speak in front of the class.

With every new accomplishment, self-confidence grows, your comfort zone expands, and your fears decrease. Where you once couldn't have imagined going into the big city alone, today you do it every day on the way to work. Where once you were a white-knuckle flyer, now you're a seasoned road warrior. We all experience a level of fear when we are about to step up our game and try something new. But we analyze the fear, we calculate the risk-reward ratio, we learn how to reduce and manage the risks, and we go for it. After mastering a new set of skills just a few times, fear has been completely replaced with confidence and you've grown into a bigger, better someone than you used to be.

Good news! You have more fearful times yet to look forward to!

As long as you continue to challenge yourself and raise the bar with new experiences, you will face at least some level of fear. If it's an invitation to go skinny-dipping with the sharks off Australia or base-jumping from the Burj Khalifa in Dubai, the fear may be intense, the risk-reward calculation unappealing, and you might decide to take a pass. But if the challenge is to apply for a promotion at work or write that book you've had in your head for years, the fears are entirely manageable and you'll feel fantastic after you've overcome them. Your fear lets you know that you are standing at the perimeter of your comfort zone. You have the choice to maintain the status quo by running back to the middle or step outside that line and grow.

Fear demands a decision about your next action.

The psychologists call it 'fight or flight' but the choice implies that you'll choose an action—run away or charge. Worry and anxiety, on the other hand, are states of inaction. Our friendly white-tail is frozen in the headlights. When you allow worry and anxiety to take over, you freeze and you stop growing.

So, now that we're comfortable with the fact that at least some level of fear will always be waiting when you try something new, what might a worry- and anxiety-free life feel like?

A worry-free person:

- Wakes up every morning looking forward to the day. They know it will include both challenges and pleasures, and they excitedly anticipate both. Their first thought recognizes the potential and the promise that the new day holds, and they can't wait to experience it. If the day is to include fresh challenges, they look forward to taking them on, learning from them, overcoming them, and feeling the self-esteem that comes with accomplishment. If the day is to include pleasures—intellectual, emotional, physical, or spiritual—they look forward to those as well, knowing that life is to be savored and enjoyed.
- Is confident that they will be able to cope with anything that is thrown at them. They aren't arrogant or cocky, but they recognize that they've

been able to meet every challenge that has ever been put in front of them. They know they are resourceful, but they also don't hesitate to ask for advice or assistance when they need it. They're creative in their problem-solving and wide open to learning new skills in the face of new challenges.
- Expects that things will work out. They are, at their core, optimistic and choose to interpret events and circumstances in a positive light. At the same time, they are realistic, knowing that there may very well be struggle, delay, and even temporary defeat involved in getting to the outcome they want. But they will view that struggle as an opportunity to learn and grow, rather than to complain and look for others to blame.
- Remains flexible. They are never so attached to their own point of view or approach to a situation that they can't consider and try something new. In fact, they love to hear and try new ideas and have little or no pride of authorship when it comes to overcoming challenges.
- Enjoys a high level of self-esteem — which is dramatically different than ego. They are confident in their abilities and comfortable with their limitations. They are aware of their own accomplishments and recognize the efforts they have gone through in order to reach their current position.

They are also aware that there is still more mountain to be climbed.
- Focuses on the wonderful aspects of their lives. They have tremendous awareness of and gratitude for all the positive things they enjoy—health, prosperity, relationships, etc.—and live in positive anticipation of improvement in the areas of their lives that aren't yet in the best of shape.
- Is highly appreciative of everything they have been given, earned, come into, or otherwise have to enjoy. They take nothing for granted and freely express their gratefulness to others. They are especially expressive of their gratitude to those who have helped or supported them in their learning and growth, whether that has been in their career, their health, or their personal development.
- Is generous to everyone and gives freely because they know that they are well supplied. They share what they have because they know that there is always more where that came from. They never see prosperity as a zero-sum game, and they understand that worrying and hoarding will always result in their own anxiety, suffering, and lack.

- Is comfortable with uncertainty. They know that trying to predict and control the world and demand that circumstances conform with their expectations will only result in exhaustion and frustration. So they don't bother. They roll with the waves that come and use their flexibility to adapt to changing situations and challenges. They recognize fear when it shows up and, rather than run from it, they use it to acquire new skills and take advantage of new opportunities.
- Is highly self-aware. They have mastered the art of self-observation—also known as mindfulness—and are intimately familiar with their own strengths and shortcomings. They don't judge themselves unworthy or undeserving, but they do constantly set and strive for new goals and higher ground.

It's entirely possible for you to become that worry-free person. It requires, first, that you want to. It will require that you put in effort and break some old habits. But it won't be as challenging or take nearly as long as you think. You've already learned how to turn your worries into dust and blow them away. Now let's begin to take steps toward that worry-free life.

In the same way that we used visualization to turn the anxiety into a mere dust ball, let's use it to imagine what your life will be like when worry is no longer your companion. We'll start small.

Nathaniel Branden was a psychotherapist and writer known for his work in the psychology of self-esteem. He said that self-esteem is "the disposition to experience oneself as competent to cope with the basic challenges of life and as worthy of happiness." He also believed that, while parents, teachers, friends, and others can nurture and support your self-esteem, if it's to be really effective, it's primarily a do-it-yourself job. So he emphasized "internally generated practices," in other words, positive self-talk.

Do you recall earlier, where we said that the first step is to take 100 percent responsibility for absolutely everything that happens to you and in your life? Rather than jumping straight to the 100 percent mark, let's use some of Nathanial Branden's work to begin with just 5 percent. Ask yourself, how might your life be different if you took just 5 percent more responsibility for it? If you decided to be just five percent less anxious?

Here are some examples:

If I were to take 5 percent more responsibility for and be 5 percent less worried about my health . . .

- I would exercise thirty minutes every day.
- I would drink soda just once per week.

- I would join the yoga class.
- I would meditate for ten minutes, five times a week.

If I were to take 5 percent more responsibility for and be 5 percent less worried about my finances . . .

- I would put 10 percent into my savings account from every paycheck.
- I would cut up half of my credit cards.
- I would eat out only twice a week.
- I would meet with a financial advisor and make a plan.

If I were to take 5 percent more responsibility for and be 5 percent less worried about my children's well-being . . .

- I would talk with them about situational awareness.
- I would avoid watching and reading scary news stories.
- I would remind myself how responsible they already are.
- I would recall how I took and survived my share of risks when I was a teenager.

If I were to take 5 percent more responsibility for and be 5 percent less worried about my career . . .

- I would take one online or evening course a year to improve my skills.
- I would invite my boss to share her goals for the division and for me.
- I would speak up more in meetings and share my ideas.
- I would raise my performance by setting new work standards for myself.

If I were to take 5 percent more responsibility for and be 5 percent less worried about social media . . .

- I would set a daily time and time limit for interacting on social media.
- I would cancel my accounts in the social media channels I find most disturbing.
- I would spend more time outdoors in nature.
- I would surround myself with positive people and disconnect from the toxic ones.

Now it's your turn. Use the following prompts and insert your own go-to worry topics to show how you would move toward becoming worry-free by making just a 5 percent change. I encourage you to write your answers in your journal, but feel free to use the form on the following pages if you prefer.

If I take 5 percent more responsibility for and be 5 percent less worried about _____

I would _____

I would _____

I would _____

I would _____

If I take 5 percent more responsibility for and be 5 percent less worried about _____

I would _____

I would _____

I would _____

I would _____

If I take 5 percent more responsibility for and be 5 percent less worried about _____

I would _____

_____

I would _____

_____

I would _____

_____

I would _____

_____

If I take 5 percent more responsibility for and be 5 percent less worried about _____

I would _____

_____

I would _____

_____

I would _____

_____

I would _____

_____

Three Keys to Your Worry-Free Life

You've now learned how to objectify your anxieties and remove them from your mind and your body. And you experienced—at least for a moment—how good it feels to be free of that chronic, nagging burden that won't let you relax and enjoy the simple pleasures of living.

The nature of a habit, though, is to want to stick around, and it won't give up and go away happily. It's unlikely that a single guided visualization will be enough to permanently rid yourself of the worry habit. It's going to require that you establish and sustain a set of new habits that will displace the old ones and empower you to become your full and authentic self.

As you transition from anxiety to worry-free, there are three major and nine minor habits that you will want to incorporate into your psyche. The more these become instinctive thought patterns in your daily life, the less worry and anxiety you will experience.

14

WORRY–FREE HABIT#1:
AN ATTITUDE OF GRATITUDE

Hoda Kotb is a journalist, television personality, and author. She is a main co-anchor of the NBC News morning show *Today*. In an interview with talk show host Andy Cohen she listed the things she does to start each day with a positive attitude.

> *When you wake up in the morning, first thing, write down three things you're grateful for. Not 'the sunrise,' or 'my health,' something very specific and different every day. The guy who held the door even though he had three bags in his hands and could have let it swing. Something small and specific. Then, after you write the three things down, write down one great thing that happened in the last 24 hours no matter how big or small. It starts to change the way you think when you wake up. Instead of 'Oh God . . . ,' your brain starts literally changing to focus on three*

good things and one great thing. The last thing is one random act of kindness. Every day.

Every person who has ever attained a level of greatness and achievement for which they are admired by the rest of the world claims gratitude as a central core in their life. Every inspirational leader, coach, or thinker whom we respect places gratitude at the top of the list of their closely held values.

It is impossible to be in a state of appreciation and fear at the same time.
—Dan Baker

When I started counting my blessings, my whole life turned around.
—Willie Nelson

Let us rise up and be thankful, for if we didn't learn a lot today, at least we learned a little, and if we didn't learn a little, at least we didn't get sick, and if we got sick, at least we didn't die; so, let us all be thankful.
—Buddha

Be thankful for what you have; you'll end up having more. If you concentrate on what you don't have, you will never, ever have enough.
—Oprah Winfrey

When you are grateful, fear disappears and abundance appears.
—Tony Robbins

The roots of all goodness lie in the soil of appreciation for goodness.
—Dalai Lama

There are only two ways to live your life. One is as though nothing is a miracle. The other is as though everything is a miracle.
—Albert Einstein

No one who achieves success does so without the help of others. The wise and confident acknowledge this help with gratitude.
—Alfred North Whitehead

I would maintain that thanks are the highest form of thought, and that gratitude is happiness doubled by wonder.
—Gilbert K. Chesterton

Gratitude is the healthiest of all human emotions. The more you express gratitude for what you have, the more likely you will have even more to express gratitude for.
—Zig Ziglar

UNSUBSCRIBE FROM ANXIETY

Some people grumble that roses have thorns; I am grateful that thorns have roses.

—Alphonse Karr

When you are worried and anxious your mind is so full of what's wrong and what seems about to get worse, that it's impossible to see the overwhelming number of things in your life that are right. We've talked about how mountain climbers and tightrope walkers are coached to never look down because it will instantly fill their minds with the consequences of failure rather than the rewards of success. Worry and anxiety do the same thing. Instead of seeing all your remarkable talents, accomplishments, and opportunities, your vision is restricted to the dreaded consequences that will befall you should things go wrong.

As with all our worrying, 'looking down' is a mental habit that can be replaced with a more constructive one. The new habit you're going to cultivate is to mentally get out in front of that downward spiral and stop it before it really gets snowballing down the hill. The best way to do this is gratitude.

If you fill your mind with all the things you have to be grateful for, there won't be any room for worrisome thoughts. This also pulls your RAS into action and it begins to find and arrange for even more things to be grateful for. By filling your mental field of vision with what you have, you will displace and replace the view of what you're afraid you might lose.

Gratitude doesn't have to mean getting down on your knees in prayer. But it does mean that, at least daily, if not regularly throughout your days, you remind yourself that the vast majority of things in your life are working out well. It means remaining mindful of all the good things that you have in your life and where they came from. It might be a little clichéd to suggest that you stop and smell the roses, but simple acts of mindfulness, taking note of the fact that you've got enough to buy a coffee, a home to come back to, and people who care about you is enough to shift your mentality away from the worries that have consumed you.

At the end of Chapter 12 we included a quote from Dale Carnegie, that said, in essence, the energy you spent worrying on things a year ago turned out to be fruitless because they worked out just fine in the end. Likewise, a year from now, you're going to be chuckling about the things you're worried about today. So why not take a twelve-month shortcut and focus your attention today on being grateful for all the things that are currently working out just fine?

While kindness should never be transactional, one of the truths in life is that, when you are grateful to someone who has done something for you, they want to do more. The opposite is also true. When you've done something for someone else and they haven't expressed their appreciation or gratitude, you become reluctant to give again the next time. People love to be appreciated. William James, who is often referred to as the "father of American psychology," said that the deepest craving of human nature is the need to be appreciated.

You might say that what's true for individuals is also true of the entire universe. Which is why it's a wise and liberating practice to be grateful for those things you have that might not have come from someone specific. Your health, your intelligence, your creativity, your ability to love others—while some of them were no doubt nurtured by your parents, your teachers, and others, none of these were handed to you by another person. Yet we are so much better off when we spend time being grateful for those gifts, regardless of how you think they originated.

Gratitude is an antidote to negative emotions, a neutralizer of envy, hostility, worry, and irritation. It is savoring; it is not taking things for granted; it is present-oriented.

—Sonja Lyubomirsky

In order to cultivate this new habit of gratitude, you might want to incorporate a number of simple practices into your daily life, at least until the habit is fully ingrained. You may find, though, that these new practices are so helpful and uplifting that you want to maintain them long after the new mental habit is well established. Practices that can help you cultivate an attitude of gratitude include:

Keep a gratitude journal

We began this chapter by relating how Hoda Kotb begins every day by writing down three things for which she's grateful and one great thing that's happened in the past twenty-four hours. If you find a special notebook and keep it by your bedside, the book will remind you each morning and the habit will be easier to maintain. I seek out journals that are beautiful and I write with a beautiful pen that was a very special gift from my wife. Simply looking at the book and the pen each day gives me a little visual gift for which I'm grateful.

Remind yourself regularly

Put a standing appointment in your calendar to pause every day, even for just two minutes, and put yourself into an appreciative state of mind. Put down what you're doing and simply look around. No matter where you are or what you're doing, there will be a long list of things within eyesight for you to appreciate. Maybe it's your work cubicle and you can be grateful for having a job. If you're driving, be grateful for your car and the gas or electricity that's propelling it. If you're at home, see the familiar surroundings that bring you such comfort.

Pick up a gratitude rock

Keep a small stone in your pocket or purse. Then, every time you see or feel it, let it trigger a moment of appreciation for where you are, what you have, and the people you love and who love you back. The tiny little tactile reminder is enough to bring appreciation to the front of your mind at numerous times through the day. Eventually you'll remember all on your own, but keep the gratitude rock anyway and be grateful for the role it played in helping you remember.

Write 'Thank You' notes

We're buried in emails, texts, and direct messages to the point where we delete them in bulk.

But when was the last time you received—or sent—a hand-written note or a card to someone? This archaic means of communication has become so rare that it's acquired a preciousness that will easily convey the sincerity of your appreciation. Get yourself some nice notecards and get into the practice of sending one each week to someone that has been kind to you, has helped you in some way, or who you simply appreciate for who they are. You'll not only make their day, they'll likely keep and smile at your card for months.

Give back

You will never repay your parents for giving you your life. Nor will your children ever be able to repay you for everything you've done for them. But that doesn't mean we shouldn't pay the favor on to someone else. Your tally will never be even and trying to make it so misses the point. We give and appreciate for the simple beauty of giving and appreciating. When someone does an act of kindness for you, say thanks by passing it along to someone else.

What are the things you should be grateful for and appreciative of?

Begin with yourself. For the fact that you're alive and breathing. For your body, regardless of the shape it's in. For your heart, lungs, liver, left foot, and little finger. For the food, water, and oxygen that sustains you. For the intelligence, the resourcefulness, and the creativity that have brought you through a challenging world. For the five senses that let you perceive, interact with, and enjoy the world around you. For your ability to read, write, speak, and wink at a friend. For your ability to know what you want and then go after it.

Then move on to those around you. For the parents who gave birth to you. For any children you may have, the love they gave as they grew up and the lessons they provided for your own growth. For any siblings you might have, regardless of the way they treated you back then. For friends who support, encourage, and stand by you. For the leaders who started the businesses and organized the agencies that employ you and provide the products and services that you need. For the life-guides who have provided your compass and helped you stay on the path you have set for yourself.

For your successes. For the swimming trophy you won in middle school and the graduate degree you achieved much later. For your ability to simply look after yourself and function in society. For the job you won and continue to excel at. For completing the online course and showing up for yoga class three weeks out of four. For overcoming your shyness and asking him out on a date. For the promotion you earned at work and the karaoke performance you gave for your friends last week.

For those who have helped you achieve those successes. For the parents who cheered you on and convinced you that you could do it. For the teachers and coaches who taught you the skills and had your back as you tentatively tried them out. For the professors and tutors who pointed the way and helped you fine-tune your path. For the authors of all the books you've read, creators of the online courses you've taken, and the YouTubers who showed you how to unclog the sink.

For everything you have. For the clothes that keep you warm, the home that shelters you, and the income that supports you. For the technology you use, the car you drive, and the toothpaste that keeps your teeth gleaming white. For your refrigerator, your dishwasher, and your voice-activated remote TV control. For the comfortable chair you're in right now and the bed that's waiting for you tonight. For the stuffed animal you've kept from childhood even if all its fur is long worn off.

If you concentrate on finding whatever is good in every situation, you will discover that your life will suddenly be filled with gratitude, a feeling that nurtures the soul.
—Rabbi Harold Kushner

15

WORRY–FREE HABIT #2: REPLACE IT WITH PURPOSE

There are two great days in a person's life—the day we are born and the day we discover why.

— Anonymous

The Greek philosopher Aristotle was apparently the originator of the saying "Nature abhors a vacuum." In other words, when there is nothing there, something else will always rush in to fill the empty space.

One of the reasons that meditation can be so challenging is that, during it, we attempt to empty our minds of all thought. Where there's a vacuum of thought, there are always plenty of other thoughts that are more than happy to rush in to fill the void. When worry has been a long-established habit, the thoughts that rush in tend to be those that make us anxious.

To counter this reaction, we need other, more important, more compelling and energizing thoughts that will rush in and fill our minds, leaving no room for worry and anxiety. So the second major key to living a worry-free life is to get in touch with and passionately pursue that which you are put on this earth to do: your life purpose.

No one was put on this earth for no particular reason. Every one of us has a calling, a reason for being, something important to accomplish. The challenge is that too many of us are content to simply roll through life, bumping from one event to the next. Or, alternatively, do the things that we believe others expect us to do because they are 'worthy,' 'practical,' 'well-paying,' or otherwise impressive. Too few of us go in search of our purpose and, finding it, set out to achieve it with every fiber of our being. Your purpose is your 'why'—why you get up in the morning, why you get excited about the things you do, why you take on challenges that are difficult.

We often hear about the life purposes of famous people. Bill Gates, for example, when he started Microsoft, said that his mission was to put "a computer on every desk and in every home." Steve Jobs, cofounder of Apple, committed himself to "make a contribution to the world by making tools for the mind that advance humankind." In 1961, John F. Kennedy changed history and mobilized an entire nation when he said, "I believe that this nation should commit itself to achieving the goal, before this decade is out, of landing a man on the moon and returning him safely to the earth."

It might be tempting to say that only famous, accomplished people have mission statements and life purposes. That 'noble missions' aren't for us mere mortals. But it's far more likely that they are famous and accomplished *because* they have mission statements and life purposes that guide them through life like a laser toward their goals.

Nor should we kid ourselves that those who accomplish great things don't face their share of fears and obstacles and have plenty that they could worry about, if they chose to.

Oprah Winfrey was born into extreme poverty and overcame immense challenges before her career caught on. A gifted communicator from earliest childhood, she has gone on to inspire millions to improve their own lives. Her stated purpose in life is "To be a teacher. And to be known for inspiring my students to be more than they thought they could be."

At the age of eight, Maya Angelou was raped by a family friend. When he was later murdered, she felt responsible and became mute for almost five years. She later wrote that "I thought, my voice killed him; I killed that man, because I told his name. And then I thought I would never speak again, because my voice would kill anyone." She went on to receive three Grammy Awards for her spoken word albums, a Pulitzer Prize nomination, the National Medal of Arts, the Presidential Medal of Freedom, and more than fifty honorary degrees. Her stated mission was "not merely to survive, but to thrive; and to do so with some passion, some compassion, some humor, and some style."

In the absence of clear and passionate purpose, our lives are too easily bumped around, blown this way and that and side-tracked on our life's journey. These distractions include the constant stream of worry and anxiety that fills our heads.

Those who have found and chosen to pursue their purpose, in contrast, are too busy and too focused to spend their precious mental energy on pointless worry.

The 1960s hit song, "Ain't No Mountain High Enough," written by Nick Ashford and Valerie Simpson, and recorded by both Marvin Gaye and Diana Ross, seems to be a love story. But, in an interview with Oprah Winfrey following Ashford's death in 2011, Simpson said that when her husband originally wrote the lyrics, "he was referring to his all-encompassing goal to one day write songs professionally." As he looked out at the New York skyscrapers, he coined the phrase 'ain't no mountain high enough' to express his conviction that absolutely nothing was going to keep him from his dream.

Despite the high-minded nature of the mission statements that we hear from some famous public figures, there is no requirement that your purpose be earth-changing. But there is a requirement that it be authentically yours. We've all met people who volunteer their time to one worthy cause or another but can't help emitting a vibe that doesn't ring true. You might be chair of the local foodbank, but if you're doing it because you feel you're supposed to or it looks good on your resume, you've missed the point.

Your passion and purpose might be to be the best flower arranger you can be. If it gives you joy, fires your imagination, and inspires you to become an even better flower arranger, then it's your purpose. If flower arranging regularly takes you into 'the zone,' in which time loses all meaning and you feel more energized at the end than at the beginning, then it's your purpose and you'd be making a huge mistake to become a doctor because your father is a doctor or a banker because it pays well. Those choices can only lead to a life full of anxiety and disappointment.

It's far more important that your purpose be authentic, genuine, and honest for you, than it be some worthy cause as judged by others. There is nothing the least bit 'worthy' about devoting your time, your energy, and your life to something about which you don't really care.

Sir Richard Branson says that his purpose is "to have fun in my journey through life and learn from my mistakes." Along the way to having fun and learning from his mistakes, he's made much greater contributions to the world than if he'd pursued a 'real job.'

If you don't know what your purpose is—and most people don't—how do you find it?

Clues to and hints about your life purpose lie in the things that bring you joy or that you feel most passionate about. The key is to commit to spending quiet time reflecting on your life, the things that bring you the most joy, and the things you find most fulfilling.

At the same time, it requires that you be brutally honest with yourself about the joy and fulfillment—or lack of them—that you receive from the things you've been doing up till now. It's very common for someone to discover that the life they've been living has been in response to what others expect of them or what they believe they "should" do.

Perhaps you really wanted to study medieval French literature in college or become a musician or a monk, but the pressure to "do something practical that can make you a good living" was overwhelming. The number of people who are "making a good living" while popping Xanax every day to mask their anxiety grows every year.

As you reflect, here are a number of questions that you can use to prompt your thinking. Use your journal to write what comes to you and don't censor any of your thoughts. Be especially wary of any answers that arise from what you think you "should" do or say or what others might expect of you. Be prepared to be surprised by what might surface when you commit to providing honest, spontaneous responses.

- What activities, people, events, hobbies, projects, etc. make you smile?
- What are your favorite things to do?
- What were your favorite things to do when you were young?
- What makes you lose track of time?
- What makes you feel great about yourself?
- What are your natural skills, abilities, and gifts?
- Who are the people who inspire you the most? These can be anyone at all whether you know them personally or not, including family, friends, authors, artists, leaders, etc.
- What are the qualities in each person that inspire you?
- What do people typically ask you for help with?

- If you had to the opportunity to teach something, what would it be?
- If you had the opportunity to get a message across to a large group of people, what would that message be?
- Who would those people be?
- What are the challenges, difficulties, and hardships you've overcome of which you're proudest?
- How did you do it?
- What are your three most closely held values?
- What are the causes in which you believe most strongly?
- When do you feel the most satisfied, at ease, or fulfilled?
- When are the times in your life that you've experienced the most joy?
- What were you doing?
- As you contemplate your answers to those last three questions, are there any common elements or themes that recur in them all?
- Fast-forward to ninety-year-old you as you reflect on your life well lived. What are the things you've achieved, the things you've acquired and the relationships that you've developed that have mattered most to you?

- If you were to die tomorrow, what would you regret not having fully done, been, or had during your life?
- Complete the sentence, "When my life is ideal I am . . ."

If you'd like to dive even deeper into discovering your life's purpose, you may want to look into *The Passion Test*. This is a process developed by Janet Bray Attwood and Chris Attwood to help you discover your passions and begin really living them. Their book, *The Passion Test: The Effortless Path to Discovering Your Life Purpose* is a *New York Times* bestseller.

Replacing your anxiety with purpose is a surefire way to eliminate worry from your life. When passion and that feeling of enthusiasm is glowing inside you, when you're surrounded by the things, activities, and people that bring you delight, you feel alive and plugged in, you lose track of time, and you're willing to do whatever is required to see the way through to your goals. Obstacles become mere annoyances instead of paralyzing anxieties.

When the things we're working on and towards make us enthusiastic and proud, we're suddenly equipped to jump any hurdle that gets in the way. If our actions and activities are in line with our passion and purpose, it's easy to find the energy to work through the challenges that inevitably arise.

Without passion and purpose, it's too easy to get stuck surviving the day-to-day challenges and obligations. When those obstacles are blocking the way to somewhere you don't even really want to go, the effort to overcome them can be just too much trouble, so our minds get stuck in that endless, mentating loop of worry and anxiety.

When your efforts are directed at achieving goals about which you're genuinely passionate, things become easier; life flows more smoothly; the people, resources, and opportunities you need naturally gravitate toward you; and you experience more success, fulfillment and joy. And much less worry and anxiety.

We hear a great deal about the importance of setting goals for ourselves. And they are certainly important. But goals are the 'what' you'll accomplish, and action plans are the 'how' you'll accomplish it. Without knowing 'why' you're bothering to accomplish these things, however, your day-to-day activities turn into little more than stirring up dust. Your purpose gives you that 'why.' With the 'why' settled, the 'what' and the 'how' fall easily into place.

If you've been alive for more than a few decades, become entrenched in career, family, mortgage, and all the things that attach themselves to us as we go through life, it might be tempting to say that it's too late for you. Finding and pursuing your life's purpose is fine when you're twenty-five, but what do you do when you wake up to it at fifty-five? Or seventy-five?

The truth is that it's never too late to discover and pursue your life's passion. The world is full of stories of people who, in their forties, fifties, and even after standard 'retirement,' found a new meaning for their lives and changed everything.

My father, who was forced to leave school at age sixteen when his father died, was a telephone repairman for twenty years. He hated every minute of it. At the age of fifty he decided that he couldn't continue. With five children and a wife, he finished his high school diploma through correspondence courses, quit his job, and went to college to get his teaching degree.

He then spent the last fifteen years of his career with a giant smile on his face as he shared his passion for mechanics with vocational high school students. The transition was challenging for sure, but finding and being able to pursue his life's purpose made it all worthwhile.

My wife has had a passion and a talent for creative writing her entire life. Convinced by well-meaning others that you can't make a living as a writer, she pursued a very successful career as a journalist. But the itch never went away and, at the age of fifty-seven, she applied for and was accepted into a master's degree program in creative writing. She's since published five books and is currently working on her fifth novel and third travel memoir. And loving every bit of it.

I've heard people object to the idea of going back to school, saying, "Do you know how old I would be when I finally finished that degree?" The answer is, "Exactly the same age as you'd be if you don't go back to school, but a lot more fulfilled."

Replace the worry, the fretting, the anxiety that fills your mind with your passionate, joyful purpose. You'll be so busy pursuing the things you love that you won't have the time or the inclination to worry about anything.

Andrew Carnegie was an American industrialist, founder of the public library system and, at one time, the richest man in the world. His stated life purpose was "To spend the first half of my life making as much money as I can—and the second half giving it away."

16

WORRY–FREE HABIT #3: INSTANT ACTION

In Chapter 4, and then again in Chapter 13, we talked about how fear, in response to a real and present danger, demands a decision about your next action. Are you going to turn tail and run? Or are you going to stand your ground and fight back? Because of the immediacy of the threat, we're forced to quickly choose which action we're going to take and then get on with it. *Now!*

Worry and anxiety, though, arise as we respond to perceived threats that are much more vague, hard to define, or somewhere off in the future. Instead of taking some kind of definitive and results-oriented action, we muddle about what's going to happen to us and what, if anything, we should do. And the muddling goes on, and on, and on.

For example, I live on the southeast coast of the US. Every year, as summer winds down, hurricane season winds up, along with the palpable anxiety that you can almost feel in the air. The problem with hurricanes is that you can see them coming for weeks ahead. It's a slow-motion threat that gives you way too much time to think about all the horrible things that might happen. Everyone is glued to their screens watching the path and strength predictions from the various weather-monitoring agencies. Are we watching the Navy Model? The American Model? The European Model? How about a conglomeration of them all? I've never inquired, but I'd be willing to bet that benzos prescriptions in the southeast spike every year from June to November.

Yet hurricanes, powerful as they can be, are pretty easy to prepare for: Have an emergency kit stocked with water, canned food, batteries, and the other essentials that are listed on countless websites. Know the evacuation route you'll take, should the order be given. Move your lawn furniture into the garage. Let your loved ones know where you're heading.

That's it. Once you've taken those actions, you can relax, have a snooze, read a book, go for a walk ... Anything but worry. Because from that point on, any anxiety that you expend is a complete waste and only makes you feel terrible, raises your blood pressure ... Well, we've been through this list before.

There's a delightful little piece called "The Serenity Prayer." Written by theologian Reinhold Niebuhr in the 1930s, it truly encompasses the perfect approach to anxiety with action:

God, grant me the serenity to accept the things I cannot change, the courage to change the things I can, and the wisdom to know the difference.

In the case of a hurricane, I can't do anything to stop it coming, but I can update the status of my emergency kit and move the furniture off my deck. Then I can stop worrying and get on with my life.

One of the characteristics of worry is that we evaluate options, alternatives, and choices over and over, endlessly weighing this against that. Then we go back and do it all again. The paralysis of anxiety bogs us down in the ceaseless cycle of analyze, plan, compare, doubt, repeat. In the face of any perceived threat, though, you have two intelligent choices: Do something or do nothing.

Doing something—anything—provides you with the benefit of results. If you get the result you want, the problem is solved. If you get a different result, you'll at least have feedback and you can fine-tune your action as you try something else. Doing nothing, on the other hand, provides you with the benefit of leisure, rest, and relaxation.

The endless analysis and mentation of the worrier, though, lies somewhere in between. It consumes tremendous energy but produces no results. And it allows no leisure, rest, or relaxation. In other words, it's the worst possible option.

Johann Wolfgang von Goethe once wrote, "Whatever you do, or dream you can, begin it. Boldness has genius and power and magic in it." There's also an old axiom of success that says, "The universe rewards action."

When you begin to take action, all manner of things begin to happen that work in your favor. The people around you recognize that you're serious and those who want the same things align and want to team with you. You produce results, which show and teach you things that you couldn't possibly learn from others, reading books, watching YouTube, or endlessly analyzing the situation. You start to get feedback about how your actions can be made better, more efficient, and faster. When you begin to take action you unleash and harness forces that you didn't even know existed.

Everyone who has ever lived has faced challenges that had the potential to be worrying. Why do some people seem to be more adept at getting past these challenges than others? In Stephen Covey's book, *The 7 Habits of Highly Effective People*, the very first habit is "Be Proactive." In other words, don't sit and wait in reactive mode. Do something.

Franklin D. Roosevelt, in the face of the Great Depression, said, "It is common sense to take a method and try it. If it fails, admit it frankly and try another. But above all, try something."

People who are consistently successful get up and do what needs to be done. They start something. Then they learn from their mistakes, make corrections, and try again. In this process they build momentum and either achieve their goals or something even better than they dreamed.

In his live seminars, Jack Canfield, co-author of the *Chicken Soup for the Soul* books and author of *The Success Principles*, shows how those who are trapped by worry and anxiety frequently stop themselves from taking action for one reason or another. He begins by holding up a hundred-dollar bill and asks if anyone in the audience would like it. Then he waits for people to take action. Many raise their hand. Some call out that they want the money. But typically there are only a few people who actually come to the stage to get the money. When they do, he gives it to them and they sit down, a hundred dollars richer for their efforts. Canfield then points out that the person with the money did something no one else did—they took the necessary action to get the hundred dollars.

Too many of us think about stepping up and taking action, but then stop ourselves for one reason or another. When Canfield asks the audience why they didn't just come up and take the bill, the answers are typically:

- I didn't want to look like I wanted or needed it that badly.
- I wasn't sure if you would really give it to me.
- I was too far back in the room.
- Other people need it more than I do.
- I didn't want to look greedy.
- I was afraid I might be doing something wrong and then people would judge me or laugh at me.
- I was waiting for further instructions.

How many of these excuses are preventing you from taking decisive action on those things that you worry about? How often has part of you wanted to get on with solving the problem, but another part of you held yourself back, waiting for a better time, waiting for more instructions or concerned that someone else might judge you? Every time that a viable action is warranted but you hesitate, delay, or fail to act, you rob yourself of a little bit of life. And you condemn yourself to the misery of more worry and anxiety.

We spend far too much time waiting for conditions to be just right before we take action. We wait for reassurance, inspiration, the right timing, the economy to improve, the kids to leave home, the rain to stop, a clear set of instructions, the alignment of the planets. I once heard it said that the best time to plant a tree was twenty-five years ago. The second-best time is right now. What, exactly, are you waiting for? Permission? Perfect conditions? Guarantees? They're not coming. So just go ahead and leap.

You may find yourself in a situation where action is needed, but you don't have the skills, knowledge, or resources to take that action yourself. In that case you need to ask for help. Which is another stumbling block that keeps so many people locked in the worry loop. None of us can do everything alone, and asking for help is a wonderful and valuable skill that the world's most successful people have mastered.

What do you need help with in order to avoid the oncoming threat that is causing you so much worry? Do you need to call someone to ask for information? Do you need to ask to borrow money? Do you need to ask for a recommendation or introduction? Do you need to ask for a job? Do you need to ask for a simple helping hand?

We live in a society that is uncomfortable with asking for help. Which is actually a bit surprising because the vast majority of people are only too happy to help us. Altruism is a natural human instinct. We're just afraid to ask. What are we afraid of? We don't want to look needy. We don't want to be judged. We don't want to feel inferior or beholden. We don't want to impose on anyone. And the more we hide behind those fears, the less we're able to accomplish and the more we stay stuck in the anxiety rut.

From now on, whenever you find yourself worrying (because you've now developed the habit of self-observation) it will serve you well to become your own action coach and ask yourself a series of questions.

1. What is it that I really want out of this situation?
2. How am I scaring myself?
3. What are the mental, emotional, or physical blocks that are holding me back from taking action on this?
4. What justifications or rationalizations am I telling myself that are keeping me from taking action on this?
5. What is one action that I can take in the next fifteen minutes that will take a positive step towards resolving this situation?
6. What are three actions that I can take in the next twenty-four hours to help resolve this situation?
7. What reward will I give myself for following through on this commitment?

8. What consequence will I impose on myself for failure to take these actions?

That's how a person with an 'Instant Action' orientation works. When they find themselves in a situation that is unpleasant or unsatisfactory they decide, right away, to do something about it. Now that you're that kind of person, what step or steps could you take, right this instant, to do something about the thing that is worrying you? Set down the book, put aside whatever else you've got going on, and take action. What will you do? Make a phone call to have that conversation? Book an appointment to get it dealt with? Schedule a meeting to address the problem? What actions will you continue to take first thing tomorrow morning?

Regardless of the situation that has you worried, concerned, or anxious, there is always something that you can do, right now, that will help alleviate your stress. And in taking that action, you will immediately feel better because you stepped outside your comfort zone. Because you did something that broke your mind out of that endless cycle of mentation. Because you took control and moved the marker further down the field.

Let's look at a couple of examples of how this might work:

You're worried about next week's doctor's appointment for your annual checkup because you haven't been eating well or exercising enough.

1. What is it that I really want out of this situation?
   A clean bill of health and the doctor smiling and telling me that every vital sign is normal and healthy.

2. How am I scaring myself?
   I am scaring myself by imagining a diagnosis of some disease brought on by poor diet and exercise habits.

3. What are the mental, emotional, or physical blocks that are holding me back from taking action on this?
   I have an aversion to exercise because I was teased in gym class; I find my couch way too comfortable; I like cake far more than vegetables.

4. What justifications or rationalizations am I telling myself that are keeping me from taking action on this?
   I'm relatively young and still in pretty good shape, so I won't have to think about this for another ten years; my mother was really healthy even though she didn't exercise regularly

5. What is one action that I can take in the next fifteen minutes that will take a positive step towards resolving this situation?

Call the health club and take out a membership.

6. What are three actions that I can take in the next twenty-four hours to help resolve this situation?
   Clean all the junk food out of my fridge; call my friend and ask to join her morning walking group; make an appointment with the personal trainer and nutritionist at the health club I just joined.

7. What reward will I give myself for following through on this commitment?
   I will allow myself one "cheat day" per week.

8. What consequence will I impose on myself for failure to take these actions?
   I will write a check for two hundred dollars to my younger sister.

You're worried that your financial records are a mess and tax season is less than a month away.

1. What is it that I really want out of this situation?
   An easy tax return with no surprises.

2. How am I scaring myself?
   I am scaring myself by imagining that I am missing important receipts and tax records, and I'll be subject to fines and penalties by the IRS.

3. What are the mental, emotional, or physical blocks that are holding me back from taking action on this?
I tell myself that financial records are boring and beneath me, but the truth is that I'm frequently just too lazy to be bothered paying attention.

4. What justifications or rationalizations am I telling myself that are keeping me from taking action on this?
I pay my accountant to look after all this, and I should reserve my brain power for more important things.

5. What is one action that I can take in the next fifteen minutes that will take a positive step towards resolving this situation?
Call my accountant and commit to having all my records, forms, and receipts to his office within seven days.

6. What are three actions that I can take in the next twenty-four hours to help resolve this situation?
Set aside this weekend to sort through all my records and receipts; go to the office supply store and buy proper filing supplies; buy a bookkeeping software package so I can input the receipts monthly.

7. What reward will I give myself for following through on this commitment?
I will use my refund check to treat myself to some new

clothes.

8. What consequence will I impose on myself for failure to take these actions?
   I will donate my entire refund check to charity.

In the face of any perceived threat, you have three choices: Do something, worry, or do nothing. Worry is completely worthless, so let's take that option off the table.

Doing something, and doing it immediately, emulates the most successful people the world has known. So analyze the situation, identify what, if anything, can be done to reduce, eliminate, or manage the threat you believe is coming and get on with it.

If, however, your analysis determines that there is absolutely nothing that can be done right now, or if you've done everything that can possibly be done for the moment, take the third option. Relax, read a book, go for a hike, play with your kids. There's nothing to worry about.

17

TEN NEW MENTAL HABITS

To remain in Victim Consciousness is to empower outside influences to dictate who you should be, what you should and should not do, and what your place is in life.

—Michael Beckwith

You are no longer a victim of your anxiety. You have chosen to opt out of the myth that it, somehow, controls you and that you have no option but to suffer the misery of nonstop worry. Congratulations, you're done with it!

Now that you've released that old logjam of thoughts and beliefs that held you in anxiety's grip, you'll want to make sure it doesn't start to jam up again. Old habits much prefer to stick around, and they'll try all manner of tricks to lure you back into worry mode. It takes some focused practice to build your new habits to the point where they're well-enough established that you'll never find yourself worrying again.

We've already introduced three major new habits of thinking that will, over time, help you create new beliefs and new behaviors. In this chapter we're going to explore ten additional, supplemental practices that will help you stay in charge of your thoughts and away from worry.

Previously, when you were taking inventory and writing about your anxieties in your journal, I asked if there was anything that acted as a trigger for your anxiety. If someone has a gluten allergy, their strategy to avoid digestive problems is simple—avoid eating anything with wheat in it and everything's good. But if you treat yourself to a baloney sandwich on Wonder Bread, don't act surprised when you find yourself heading to the bathroom. In the same way, if you want your worry-free life to continue, you're going to have to avoid those people, events, and circumstances that are guaranteed to get you on a high-rolling boil again.

Try implementing these new lifestyles to edge out the old habits. If you want, think of them as maintenance to avoid backsliding.

1. Quit the complaining club

You know them. They're the ones who phone you up regularly, and it's always bad news. "Did you hear about the earthquake?!!" "Looks like it's going to rain again today." "I bet the traffic is going to be bad this morning." Misery does love company, but it doesn't have to be you. Drop out of the worry club. Avoid the people who drag you down and seek out the ones who lift you up and make you feel alive. And in those times when you can't avoid the 'worry-monger,' keep the chat short and follow it immediately with a little treat for yourself. As Mel Robbins says, "toxic people are still toxic, even when they're disguised as family."

There are people in your life who can simply walk into the room and you're completely drained of energy. They bring the tension, the stress, and the anxiety with them, and they're more than happy to share it around. But there are others in your life too. They're the ones who always leave you feeling better than you did before they came. They bring the energy, the enthusiasm, the optimism, and the encouragement.

All emotions can be contagious. Run from the toxic ones and seek out and breathe deeply from the uplifting ones.

2. Avoid the news

Walk through an airport, run on a treadmill at the gym, or sit down for a drink at the bar and there it is—nonstop news. You can't even escape it at 35,000 feet. I'm writing this very paragraph on a plane headed for Seattle. Two rows ahead of me and across the aisle, someone has chosen to watch, not one of the forty-seven movies available for free, not a soothing or uplifting concert or an exciting sports game, but CNN's 24/7 live satellite streaming of the latest horrific events around the world and right here at home.

We've become addicted to it, and the networks, the newspapers, the podcasters, the bloggers, and social media have all drunk the Kool-Aid. News stations make their money from the number of eyeballs and eardrums that are tuned in, and the more sensational, the more terrifying they can make the report, the more fearful we become and the more we tune in.

But you don't have to! There is no need whatsoever for you to know—*right now!*—what's going on at the latest G7 summit or that another royal has had another baby. At most, give yourself a once-a-day, quick summation of the headlines. Better still, try going without the news for an entire week and see how much lighter, freer, easier you feel! Trust me, there is nothing on the news that you need to know.

3. Stay away from social media

If the news is addicting, social media is crack cocaine. It's no surprise that social media is a significant part of the reason we're seeing such a rapid rise in anxiety and depression and the use of prescription drugs to treat it. When it comes to anxiety, we voluntarily put ourselves into what can be one of the most venomous situations possible. And we stay there, breathing the toxic fumes, all day, every day.

Two of the most common causes of anxiety are the perception of being judged by others and negative judgement of ourselves. One of the running jokes of social media is how everyone else's life always appears so perfect when compared to our own. Of course, somewhere deep inside we know (or at least we hope) that it's not true, but in the instant of an Instagram story about all the fun they're having while you're at home alone, our inner critic goes into overdrive. To make matters worse, any notion of social filters, civility, or kindness seems to be left behind when those 280 characters are let loose.

Facebook, Twitter, Instagram, the whole social media tidal wave has got us plugged in twenty-four-hours a day. We become addicted to the emotional roller-coaster and our blood pressure goes up and down right along with it. If you must be connected (and there's no rule that says you must) set a specific (and short!) time each day to check your phone. Then put it down and go back to that great book or your gardening, or sit for your daily ten-minute meditation.

4. Seek out uplifting entertainment

One of the great ways to improve your mood, build your self-esteem, and feel good about yourself is to indulge in a little "me-time" at the movies. Because movies are stories, our human nature connects with and learns from them in ways that can have lasting effects on how we see the world, each other, and ourselves.

What's the opposite of a 'feel-good' movie? It's one that makes you feel miserable, scared, depressed, anxious, or otherwise yucky. Same goes for music lyrics. If you're choosing to unsubscribe from anxiety, you might want to make some adjustments to your entertainment diet. While those 'feel-good' movies might have a reputation for being lightweight and occasionally a bit cheesy, the endorphins, dopamine, and serotonin pulsing through your veins will more than make up for it.

I'll happily and proudly bawl my eyes out at a rom-com or anything that Pixar wants to put out all day long. Ignore that 'I-should-watch-something-more-sophisticated' voice in your head and indulge your inner child. Ignore the 'aren't-I-so-cultured-and-urbane' movie reviewers too. What do they know about giggling!? Just pick a movie that's just fun, makes you laugh, and leaves you feeling good. The only person judging your cinematic selection is you, so give yourself a two-hour vacation and let a feel-good movie restore your soul!

Make it a habit to treat yourself to a once-a-week movie. It can be wonderful, effective, and very inexpensive therapy if your joy is running low and your confidence is hiding in the closet.

5. Appreciate yourself!

The opposites of worry and anxiety are confidence and self-esteem, and these become stronger and more robust with every one of your achievements To maintain your worry and anxiety as a harmless dust ball, it's vital that you celebrate, appreciate, and honor yourself every single day.

This isn't bragging or boasting, it's being aware of the facts. The fact that you are really good at bookkeeping, basketball, or basket-weaving is something that you should freely and proudly admit to yourself. And others when it's appropriate.

To appreciate yourself regularly and get comfortable with the fact that you're pretty darn good, write at least weekly in your journal about:

- An element of your job performance that you're proud of
- A skill you've acquired that you're proud of
- An aspect of your personal life that you're proud of
- A kindness that you've done for someone else that you're proud of

These are just suggestions. Feel free to write about anything that you're proud of. Make sure that you begin each statement with, "I am proud that I . . ."

Also use your journal to keep a 'Victory Log.' This is where you'll write down your successes at the end of each day. They don't have to be earth-shaking. In fact, it's the continuous stream of simple victories that build a solid foundation of confidence and self-esteem. So write in your journal that you balanced your checkbook, remembered to call your mother, fit into jeans that are one size smaller, cleaned out your inbox, or exercised for thirty minutes. Whenever you feel that anxiety might be trying to sneak in the back door, review your Victory Log and feel the boost. If you've managed to accomplish all that, whatever's coming at you now will be a breeze.

6. Set measurable goals

In Chapter 15 we talked about the importance of having a clear life purpose—of identifying the 'why' of your life. With your 'why' clearly understood, it's important to then lay out the 'what' by setting clear and measurable goals.

Goal-setting is one of the traits that sets high achievers apart from everyone else. Not only do they regularly set goals, they actively and doggedly pursue the achievement of them. This is one of the ways you can take 100 percent responsibility for your life and everything in it.

Most people fail to set goals. Why? Perhaps it was never modeled by their parents. It certainly wasn't taught in school. And goal-setting carries with it the risk of embarrassment and ridicule if you fall short. Safer to just avoid setting them in the first place. But successful people know that, without goals, they're adrift and rudderless.

Be sure to distinguish between goals and mere wishes. A goal has a number of very distinct traits.

- It is specific, measurable and written.
- It is believable to you.
- It is communicated to others.
- It has a time limit.
- Internal and external roadblocks are accepted as a natural part of the journey and are dealt with positively.

Set goals in every area of your life, and especially in those areas in which you have faced the greatest worry and anxiety. A set of solid goals that inspire you to action will steamroller right over any worries, anxieties, or obstacles that might dare to get in the way.

7. Visualize yourself fearlessly achieving those goals

Do you recall our little experiment with the imaginary lemon? Using nothing more than your mind and your imagination, you managed to create a reality that your body responded to physically. When you think about it, that's pretty remarkable. It also highlights the power of visualization in the achievement of your goals.

Visualization works on your behalf in three ways. First, it exercises and activates the creative powers of your subconscious mind. Second, it puts your RAS to work, which focuses your brain to seek out and find those things that support and move you toward what you're visualizing. Finally, it magnetizes and attracts you to the people, resources, and opportunities you need to achieve your goal.

The essence of visualization is to close your eyes and 'see' your goals as already complete. This is the tricky part because your logical brain keeps wanting to shout, "But my goal isn't complete! I can't lie to myself!" Every time an architect prepares a set of plans, they visualize the building as complete. Even though there's nothing but an empty, weed-filled lot, there is also a set of drawings that show a beautiful new building. With that set of drawings, with the imagination of the designer, the weed-filled lot becomes—really, actually turns into—the beautiful building. Let your imagination and your ability to visualize what doesn't yet exist turn your life into that exquisite vision. Your ability to visualize is the most underutilized success tool you possess.

8. Affirm your fearlessness daily

Where visualization uses your imagination to picture the outcomes you want to achieve, affirmations harness the energy of your words to reinforce and support the journey to your goals. An affirmation is a positive statement that declares your desired outcome as if it has already been achieved.

One of the most significant obstacles that holds us back from making big changes in our lives is the beliefs that we carry around in our heads. Those beliefs come out in the self-talk we hear all day long. "I am a worrier. My mother and my sisters are worriers. I guess it's just in my genes to worry." That belief, reinforced by years of affirming it to yourself day after day, has convinced you that you have to worry about everything. Your behavior conforms to your conviction.

When you introduce a different self-image by way of an affirmation, you interrupt the pattern and create the internal motivation that you need to achieve the goal. "I always and easily handle life's challenges with calmness, logic, and appropriate action."

Of course, at first, you don't believe yourself for a moment. But the internal dissonance that you've created begins to erode the previous belief. When you link and reinforce the new affirmation with a visual image of your desired outcome, the power to change grows even stronger. Repeat your affirmation—with feeling!—three times each day and not only will you transform your inner beliefs about yourself, you'll see your external behavior changing to match.

9. Focus on your successes

Near the beginning of this book we did an exercise in which I asked you to remember, write about, and recall the feelings associated with your successes. You were to list five successes, victories, or accomplishments you achieved before you turned eighteen, in college or at your first job, and just last week. For some people this is a very challenging exercise because they're so focused on what has or is going wrong they can't see what's going right.

Fearlessness is built on self-esteem, and self-esteem is built on accomplishment. If you never pay any attention to your accomplishments, your self-esteem has no chance to establish itself and grow to become healthy and robust. I've heard people protest by saying that they don't want to become egotistical, self-centered, and bragging. Of course you don't. But don't let that be an excuse for failing to rid yourself of anxiety for good. There's a long distance between being a chronic worrier and being arrogant and big-headed. The mindfulness you've been developing during this process will guarantee that you never go too far in the other direction.

Earlier in this chapter I suggested that you use your journal to maintain a Victory Log of all your successes. When you keep track of the remarkable things you accomplish on this journey through life, you get a different, much more accurate, picture of what a strong, capable person you actually are.

10. Meditate daily

There are many things you can do, many habits you can take up, many books you can read and many practices you can begin on the way to transforming yourself. There isn't one of them that will transform you more quickly or more positively than the daily practice of meditation.

We've spent this entire book learning that worry and anxiety are the product of useless and destructive mental habits. They are the result of our minds controlling us rather than us controlling it.

Meditation is a process through which you not only become intimately familiar with the workings of your mind, you gradually assume control of it and gain the ability to use it to your best advantage. Rather than being a victim of an uncontrolled mind that is easily blown off course by every breaking news flash, you become the one in charge of this incredibly powerful resource.

There is no shortage of resources for learning how to meditate, and I won't attempt to dive into the subject here. But I will reassure you of several things. First, there is no need to go into a cave or monastery. I find my living room couch to be a perfect setting. Second, don't expect to be able to sit in quiet meditation for an hour or more. Begin by just sitting quietly for two minutes. Then do it again tomorrow. Prepare to be amused by how unwilling your mind is to being placed under control. It's a wily character that does not like to give up easily. But slowly you'll discover that you want to extend the two minutes to five. The five to ten, and then ten to twenty. It won't be long before you'll look forward to it each day. And not long after that you'll depend on it.

The day you realize that you haven't worried about anything for weeks is the day you'll realize that you're now the one in charge of that remarkable, powerful, beautiful mind of yours.

18
WHAT'S NEXT

At the very beginning of this book I made you four promises. I'd like to believe that I've fulfilled each one, but it will be worthwhile to review what we've accomplished together, see if I'm right, and then talk about what happens next.

1. *I promised to show you that fear, anxiety, and worry are debilitating, yet highly removable, roadblocks that are preventing you from living your best life possible.*

The world around us is working overtime to convince us that worry, fear, and anxiety are not only a natural state of being, they're required for survival.

The reasons why the world is trying so hard to burden you with such unease are varied: The network and cable stations want to increase the number of eyeballs glued to the screen. Social media influencers are in a race to win the highest number of followers. Friends and family members have already frightened themselves silly and they just want company. Everybody has their own motive, but you can safely ignore them all.

In addition to those who are actively trying to worry you sick, we have a built-in biological 'negativity bias,' which was designed to protect you from a saber-tooth tiger attack, not a Twitter attack. But you're intelligent and aware enough to think your way through that. You don't need your appendix anymore, either.

If we give in to all these co-conspirators, we spend far too much time worrying about the horrid things that might happen to us and not nearly enough time imagining and going after all the wonderful things that are far more likely to occur.

While there are some who might argue that there are benefits to worrying—demonstrating care, solving problems, staying motivated, or some odd way of making good news seem even better, the downside of anxiety can literally kill you.

At its most benign, it feels awful, robs you of sleep, and accomplishes absolutely nothing towards resolving the issue you're facing. When it really gets cranking, you can count on anxiety as the source of high blood pressure, ulcers, heart attacks, panic attacks, gastrointestinal problems, depression, and sexual dysfunction.

But the real tragedy of allowing worry and anxiety to rule your world is that it completely undermines our enormous human potential. Our dreams shrink or disappear, our performance is weakened, and our ability to create the futures we're capable of imagining withers. In the face of our worries, we believe less, we try less, and we become less.

2. *I promised to show you that anxiety and worry are simply mental and emotional choices that have become habits and that you are fully capable of replacing those habits with healthier, more constructive ones.*

If worry and anxiety were, like aging, a fact of life over which we had no control, it would make complete sense to develop medications to treat and control them. And it's true that, for a small percentage of the population, a genuine mental illness exists that can only be treated by medical professionals. But the vast majority of those who experience anxiety are fully capable of letting it go of their own accord.

The primary obstacle that prevents many people from simply choosing to unsubscribe from anxiety is that they don't realize this option is available.

From earliest childhood and, in some cases, even prenatally, we've been exposed to and trained by parents, teachers, coaches, and countless others in authority, all of whom have also believed that worry is a fact of life. Why? Because they, too, were trained to worry by their parents and teachers. We've been passing anxiety down through the generations for so long that you'd think it was some kind of precious family heirloom to be treasured and protected. We've also got built-in reinforcement through our reticular activating systems and the law of attraction that combine to encourage and continue the behaviors and beliefs we focus on.

The fact is, though, that it's nothing more than a habitual mode of thinking that we've practiced all our lives. No one has ever thought to question whether or not it's a good idea. Once we begin to challenge the assumptions about worry, though, we discover that, like any other bad habit, it can be replaced with habits that are far healthier and more beneficial. Like any ingrained habit, it will take some effort to replace. But that effort is miniscule compared to the cost of a lifetime of anxiety. Also, like any ingrained habit, the first step to replacing it is becoming aware of your current behavior and having the desire to change.

3. *I promised to show you how you can control your anxiety instead of it controlling you.*

The first bold step toward opting out of this debilitating myth is to take 100 percent responsibility for absolutely everything that happens to you and in your life. This is a radical move because society takes tremendous delight in finding and blaming culprits for all the ills that befall us. But as long as we assign blame for our troubles to someone or something else, we surrender any power we have to change things for the better. Taking full responsibility for your own state of mind and your own success puts the control back in your hands.

While there are no doubt some situations in which you find yourself with few, if any, good choices, there is never a time when you don't have control over your thoughts and the attitude you bring to that situation. Using the formula $E + R = O$, or Event + Response = Outcome, we realize that we always have the power to choose our mental and emotional response to any event. In other words, you can blame the event (E) for your circumstances and your anxiety, or you can change your response (R) to the event (E) until you get the outcome (O) you want.

Once you've decided to take personal responsibility, you need to become intimately familiar with what it is you're taking responsibility for. You need to become an objective, third-party observer of your thoughts, feelings, and self-talk and learn how it is that you're scaring yourself. A detailed 'inventory' of your anxieties, complete with analysis of their origins, triggers, and intensities, all recorded in your journal, contributes to that impassive, scientist-like attitude and helps you distance and detach yourself from them.

Having detached yourself from your anxieties, you can begin to see them almost as objects that can be manipulated at your will. Using guided visualization, you take control of the worry-objects, commanding and directing them as you wish. The anxiety has completely lost its power over you, and you easily direct it to simply dissolve. Should you find yourself falling back into the old habit of worry-thought, you can repeat the guided visualization and be rid of it again.

4. *I promised to give you proven, practical steps that will let you live the life you've always wanted to live.*

Fear is a natural and healthy response to a perceived threat. It prompts immediate and decisive action that avoids or mitigates the danger. As we grow, facing and overcoming assorted threats, our confidence in our ability to overcome various perils grows and our fears decline.

Accomplishment builds self-esteem, and the confident person trusts their ability to respond appropriately to a threat when and if it becomes necessary. But they do not waste their time and energy worrying about a vague threat that may or may not become real.

A worry-free life is built on three major principles. First, the worry-free person is continuously and joyously grateful for the countless gifts in their life. They're aware that nasty stuff happens, but they choose to focus on the endless stream of blessings, big and small, that pour into their lives.

Second, they replace anxiety with purpose. They seek out and embrace the 'why' of their life and pursue that with passion. As a result, they have neither the time nor the interest to worry about vague threats that may or may not come about.

Finally, they adopt the practice of 'instant action.' Should something present itself that requires their attention, they turn their complete focus to solving that problem; they analyze, weigh, and choose the options that seem best in the moment; and then they act. If the action gets the wanted result, the problem is solved. If it doesn't, they assess the feedback, adjust, and act again. But they waste not one single moment in worry because they know that it accomplishes nothing.

Worry-free people also adopt a set of ten thought habits that keep their minds clear, their dispositions happy, and their ability to react ready.

These thinking habits are:
1. They resign their Complaining Club membership.
2. They actively avoid the news

3. They severely restrict their intake of social media
4. They seek out uplifting sources of entertainment
5. They actively and continuously appreciate their own abilities and accomplishments
6. They set specific, measurable, and written goals
7. They regularly visualize themselves achieving those goals
8. They use powerful affirmations to reinforce their progress toward their goals
9. They remain focused on their successes
10. They have a daily practice of meditation

I also provided a fifth, bonus promise: I promised that, if you follow these steps in a committed way, your worry and anxiety will diminish.

If you have read the book carefully and worked with the suggestions and exercises, it's likely that you are already feeling less anxious and less worried than you did at the beginning. You have already made the decision to unsubscribe from anxiety and opt out of that tired, dumb old myth that worry is simply something you have to live with.

Where you go from here and the degree to which you remain anxiety-free is up to you. I can assure you, from personal experience, that it is entirely possible to go from a worry-filled life to one that is day after glorious day of delightful adventures.

I wake up every morning knowing what I'm here to accomplish. I have a set of specific, written, and measurable goals that take me ever-closer to the finish line. And every time I get to one finish line, I gain a new perspective that allows me to set new goals for reaching the next.

Does stuff still happen along the way? You bet it does! Some of it is annoying, some a little scary, some downright challenging. But after six-and-a-half decades of overcoming challenges, I know that, one way or another, I'll be able to cope with whatever life wants to throw at me. And, after I've climbed over that obstacle, I'll have learned another lesson that I can add to my resource collection. They say that the fun lies in the journey, not the destination. I quite enjoy both.

What would you do tomorrow morning if you woke up absolutely free of worry and anxiety? What would you be thinking about? What would you decide to do? What would you set out to do knowing that you weren't the least bit afraid to fail, succeed, change, be judged, look foolish, say 'no,' or try to do something completely different?

There *is* a world that is free from worry and anxiety. And it's yours to claim if you choose.

ACKNOWLEDGEMENTS

I didn't actually write this book. Yes, I typed all the words and organized the chapters, but I can't begin to take credit for the ideas, the knowledge, and the wisdom that are contained in it. Those, I got from a thousand different people, experiences, and aha! moments. It took a big team to write this book. I'd like to acknowledge just a few of the really important members.

- *My dear wife, best friend, and perfect partner, Gail Hulnick, who miraculously continues to believe in me*
- *The wonderfully supportive folks at WindWord Group Publishing and Media*
- *My meticulous editor, Kristen Tate*
- *My advisory team, including Michael, Emeralda, Angela, Ray, The Coach, and David*
- *The incredible teachers, guides and authors who so generously poured their wisdom into books, podcasts, postings, and courses of their own, from whom I've learned so much, including:*

Esther and Jerry Hicks and Abraham
Michael Beckwith
Claude M. Bristol

Richard Bach
Sir Richard Branson
Eric Butterworth

Rhonda Byrne *H. Emilie Cady*
Jack Canfield *Julia Cameron*
Sonia Choquette *Dr. Wayne Dyer*
Charles Fillmore *Emmet Fox*
Louise Hay *Byron Katie*
Prentice Mulford *Catherine Ponder*
John Randolph Price *Bob Proctor*
Tony Robbins *Sanaya Roman*
David J. Schwartz *Ron Scolastico*
Florence Scovel Shinn *Tosha Silver*
Stuart Wilde *Oprah Winfrey*

ABOUT THE AUTHOR

Yeah, I wrote this part myself, as all authors do, even though they always write it in the second person.

- I'm old enough for Medicare, but I self-identify as a teenager who is proudly one-quarter pirate.
- I've been a successful architect, entrepreneur, and master marketer.
- I remain a wannabe painter and pianist.
- At the age of fifty-five, I ran smack into a brick wall life crisis and was forced to admit that 'my way' was not working. I set out to find a better way—and did.
- My life purpose is to know myself.
- My other life purpose now is to show and teach others how to transcend fear, worry, anxiety, and self-doubt, so that they too can pursue their limitless human potential.
- I'm told that I'm an inspiring and engaging speaker with a gift for making tough topics accessible and helping people actually enjoy the expansion of their comfort zones.
- I firmly believe that your parachute can't open till after you've jumped out of the plane.

www.ingramcontent.com/pod-product-compliance
Lightning Source LLC
Chambersburg PA
CBHW030051100526
44591CB00008B/96